Preserving

America's Past

Prepared by the Special Publications Division
National Geographic Society, Washington, D. C.

Preserving America's Past

Contributing Authors: LESLIE ALLEN, TOM MELHAM, H. ROBERT MORRISON, GENE S. STUART

Contributing Photographers: JOSEPH H. BAILEY, NATHAN BENN, IRA BLOCK, TERRY EILER, ANNIE GRIFFITHS, ETHAN HOFFMAN, STEPHANIE MAZE

Published by
The National Geographic Society
GILBERT M. GROSVENOR, *President*
MELVIN M. PAYNE, *Chairman of the Board*
OWEN R. ANDERSON, *Executive Vice President*
ROBERT L. BREEDEN, *Vice President, Publications and Educational Media*

Prepared by
The Special Publications Division
DONALD J. CRUMP, *Editor*
PHILIP B. SILCOTT, *Associate Editor*
WILLIAM L. ALLEN, WILLIAM R. GRAY, *Senior Editors*

Staff for this book
SEYMOUR L. FISHBEIN, *Managing Editor*
JOHN G. AGNONE, *Picture Editor*
CINDA ROSE, *Art Director*
JODY BOLT, *Consulting Art Director*
PALMER GRAHAM, *Senior Researcher*
MONIQUE F. EINHORN, PATRICIA F. FRAKES, SALLIE M. GREENWOOD, LOUISA V. MAGZANIAN, *Researchers*
BARBARA L. GRAZZINI, *Project Editor*
LESLIE ALLEN, RICHARD M. CRUM, THOMAS O'NEILL, GENE S. STUART, *Picture Legend Writers*

Engraving, Printing, and Product Manufacture
ROBERT W. MESSER, *Manager;*
GEORGE V. WHITE, *Production Manager;*
MARK R. DUNLEVY, *Production Project Manager;* RICHARD A. McCLURE, DAVID V. SHOWERS, GREGORY STORER, *Assistant Production Managers*
KATHERINE H. DONOHUE, *Senior Production Assistant;* MARY A. BENNETT, *Production Assistant;* JULIA F. WARNER, *Production Staff Assistant*

NANCY F. BERRY, C. REBECCA BITTLE, PAMELA A. BLACK, NETTIE BURKE, JANE H. BUXTON, MARY ELIZABETH DAVIS, CLAIRE M. DOIG, JANET A. DUSTIN, ROSAMUND GARNER, VICTORIA D. GARRETT, JANE R. HALPIN, NANCY J. HARVEY, JOAN HURST, ARTEMIS S. LAMPATHAKIS, KATHERINE R. LEITCH, VIRGINIA W. McCOY, MARY EVELYN McKINNEY, CLEO E. PETROFF, VICTORIA I. PISCOPO, TAMMY PRESLEY, SHERYL A. PROHOVICH, CAROL A. ROCHELEAU, KATHLEEN T. SHEA, KATHERYN M. SLOCUM, JENNY TAKACS, CAROLE L. TYLER, *Staff Assistants*
MICHAEL G. YOUNG, *Index*

Library of Congress CIP Data: page 196.

Ancestor of locomotives that helped spawn the railroad age in America, the John Bull *builds up a head of steam for its 150th birthday in 1981. The world's oldest steam engine in operating condition celebrated by chugging along a bit of track in Washington, D. C.* PRECEDING PAGES: *Antebellum verandas catch the harbor fog in Charleston, South Carolina. Confederate shelling of Fort Sumter in 1861 shook many of these South Battery showplaces.* PAGE 1: *Brick dwellings that housed artisans and mariners in the 1700s make Elfreth's Alley the oldest continuously occupied street in Philadelphia.* HARDCOVER: *The Victorian beachfront at Cape May, New Jersey.*

ABOVE: CIRAMA/MICHAEL LAWTON. PRECEDING PAGES: NATHAN BENN. PAGE 1: STEPHANIE MAZE. HARDCOVER: CINDA ROSE FROM PHOTOGRAPH BY STEPHANIE MAZE

Vision of yesteryear, the Wheelmen rally on Mackinac Island, Michigan. Garbed in cycling breeches,

a Living Past

By Gene S. Stuart

STEPHANIL MAZE

club members relive the 1880s, heyday of the high-wheeler bicycles.

To grow up among relatives who reminisce, tell of old happenings time and time again, recite births, deaths, and kinships like litanies, is to know a seamless survival of memories—collective memories so often heard that a child's short span of history lengthens and evolves into We instead of I.

We played checkers, my mother and I, on the checkerboard her grandfather crafted to take to war. She opened the delicate latches, took out the worn, faded pieces, and laid the old case flat, game side up. As we began, she told me stories she had been told, of how Vandiver Thompson left his family for the Civil War and marched away as a Confederate soldier. During the war he and his captain maintained a rivalry for checker championship. In those lulls when combat subsided, the two warriors faced one another across the red and black squares to battle with painted wooden disks. My mother taught me to crown kings, defend, attack, and capture.

Union soldiers wounded and captured my great-grandfather at Chickamauga. There he lost one checker, either in battle or during his removal march northward. With time, distance, and delirium, his grief grew intense and focused on the vanished checker. In a Philadelphia hospital an understanding Union nurse gave the distraught prisoner a replacement. Then, at war's end, his wooden armies again intact, he walked home to South Carolina on one leg and a crutch with his beloved checkerboard tucked under his arm. I always chose to play with the black checkers.

One of them is slightly larger than the others.

I never knew my great-grandfather, but Bess B. Walcott of Tuskegee Institute, Alabama, knew hers. In recalling him, her family memory reaches back into the 1700s—virtually the entire span of the nation's history.

Mrs. Walcott is a short woman with green eyes, pale skin, and silky white hair combed up into a French twist. Her features are still attractive, a combination of black and white ancestry. She speaks with keen memory, sharp intelligence, and great confidence, and in her 96th year I sat with her one morning as she recalled, "My great-grandfather, William Bizzell, was born sometime in the late 1700s. He always spoke with an accent. We think he came from Scotland as a stowaway. At any rate, he was a sailor. He fought with Oliver Hazard Perry in the Battle of Lake Erie during the War of 1812. In Barbados he met the woman who was my great-grandmother and brought her to this country. I remember him well. He idolized Perry, worshiped him. He named his son, my mother's father, Perry. We've kept the tradition alive. We have great-grandchildren coming along named Perry."

Bess was born in the town of Xenia, Ohio; she recalled it as a "perfect United Nations" of immigrant families. "The children thought of themselves as Italian, German, or whatever," she went on. "To them I was a true American. I was the only one who had a great-grandfather in the War of 1812. And on Decoration Day, I was the only one with two grandfathers marching in the parade. Both served as Union soldiers in the Civil War."

Weaver's art completes the work of fleecing and spinning at Middleton Place, a South Carolina landmark owned by the same family since the early 1700s. Undaunted by Civil War burning, owners revived the house, its storied gardens, and the plantation skills of an earlier day.

Rousing "Yankee Doodle" paces the fife and drum corps at Colonial Williamsburg, restored capital of 18th-century Virginia.

FOLLOWING PAGES: *Thatched huts, airy wattle fences, detail the fragile dawn of Jamestown in*

Bess Walcott sustains history in her memories of family and region, but she lives it in her surroundings. In 1908 she became a librarian at Tuskegee Institute. Booker T. Washington, who had come from slavery to establish Tuskegee as a center for black education, was its president. Later, she also worked with George Washington Carver, who spent a lifetime in agricultural research aimed at improving the plight of southern farmers.

Amid burgeoning interest in ethnic history, young people listen intently to her recollections. That morning, Troy Lissimore, superintendent of the Tuskegee Institute National Historic Site, a unit of the National Park Service, joined us. I listened to the two of them speak of Washington and Carver—she from personal experience, Troy from vivid impressions gained from older people like her.

Tuskegee and Bess Walcott represent two fascinating trails in the pursuit of America's past. Historic sites and parks evoke great lives, noted landmarks, or crucial moments in the national adventure.

For this book my colleagues and I mainly followed the other trail, where the past may live in a memory such as Bess Walcott's; where farmsteads preserve the folkways of pioneer days, a sense of the challenge of the untamed land; where old cities recapture the look of their youth—and its vigor and promise as well; where ships and cars and airplanes— many redeemed from scrap heaps—sail and sputter and flutter with antique charm.

"Tuskegee," said Bess Walcott, "was founded in 1881 to train teachers. The people who came were so far back on the other side of Now. Mr. Washington had to get them ready for Now and for the change he knew would come."

As we talked, she occasionally fell silent, a pensive look in her eyes. She held years of memories to tell me in only one morning— her We of family in the 18th and 19th centuries, her We of Tuskegee's great leaders in the early years of the 20th, her We of young Perrys coming along. I saw Bess Walcott as a living continuum from the past to the future. From her serene present she looks backward affectionately, then forward confidently.

Troy, military sharp and warmly hospitable, showed me the campus: the white frame buildings of Washington's earliest school, the sturdy brick structures of later periods.

"The Park Service and Institute administer about 26 historic buildings jointly," he said. "All date from Washington's time or shortly after, at least 60 years ago." Some are renovated, but others, no longer serviceable, may be subject to removal, Troy added.

Glass shattered and crashed to the ground. Workers at one of the buildings due to be razed were getting help from little boys lobbing volleys of stones. I wondered if they would ever again be allowed such pleasures with grown-up permission. For a moment I longed to abandon my notebook and test my ability to impress peers with exaggerated windups. But, of course, there was a serious side to the scene. Many preservationists would look upon it with despair; for them, preservation has but one goal: to preserve.

Nearby, engineers recorded the building with photogrammetry equipment to obtain an accurate, detailed record of the structure. In the future, Troy explained, if someone wants to reconstruct the razed building, he can do so, though it will be gone. I could hear both pride and regret in the superintendent's voice.

A group of young workers busily sawed and

1607; it commemorates the first permanent English settlement in America. Jamestown and nearby Williamsburg represent a style of preservation: the museum village that re-creates the look and lifeway of sites emblazoned in history.

Living Museums
Recapture Colonial Past

hammered in a frame cottage of Victorian style, restoring it from foundation to roof. The house, built by Tuskegee students in 1897, had fallen into disuse. "These young people are doing something that will have repercussions on the future," said Troy. "In time, they can come back and say, 'We didn't build it, but we saved it.' We hope they gain a sense of history and tradition."

Americans have had, from the nation's beginning, a sense of tradition, from roots in older worlds to an awareness of what makes our past distinctly American. But it was not until the mid-19th century that private citizens first joined together to save a historic house. Chroniclers of the preservation movement usually cite the campaign of Ann Pamela Cunningham and the Mount Vernon Ladies' Association of the Union as the earliest major effort. Just before the Civil War the association raised money to buy the home of George Washington—and the association still owns and cares for the Virginia shrine.

Saving historic houses remained the major focus of preservation through the rest of the 19th century and into the 20th. With the economic depression of the 1930s, the nation began to probe deeply into its heritage. In the past, somewhere, lay the American dream, bright, full of promise.

People looked backward and liked what they saw—in the folkways of an earlier America and in its architecture. In city after city decaying old neighborhoods—some dating back to colonial times—found strong voices for preservation. And the handsome old houses would be more than mere symbols of the past. "Americans were learning to define

history in a new way," wrote preservation historian Charles B. Hosmer, Jr. "It was to be a part of their living environment, not merely a museum exhibit that somehow should inspire patriotism through a connection with a great person or event."

By the 1930s the example of Colonial Williamsburg had begun to inspire preservationists across the land. Here at the site of Virginia's colonial capital the largest restoration project in the nation had been under way since 1926, combining massive research, Rockefeller family philanthropy, and the single-minded dream of the Reverend W.A.R. Goodwin. This crusading educator believed modern development at Williamsburg threatened to kill the "spirit of the past" that "haunts and hallows the ancient city and the homes of its honored dead."

His dream is reality, and Americans and visitors from around the world come to see the restored 18th-century town—the streetscapes, the facades, the interiors and furnishings, the colonial crafts, and some of the rounds of daily life. And the Colonial Parkway links it to two nearby landmarks—Jamestown, where in 1607 England achieved her first permanent settlement in the New World, and Yorktown, where the surrender of Cornwallis in 1781 ended the war that ended England's reign over the 13 Colonies.

Williamsburg, according to one scholar, represents the most complete, most competent, and most skillful effort of its kind and time. Little wonder that it served as a beacon to a growing band—custodians of publicly owned historic sites, owners of famous houses, and preservers of decaying neighborhoods. In 1949 the National Trust for Historic Preservation *(Continued on page 17)*

*Pride of the preservation
movement, Williamsburg
emerges once again as the
hub of an 18th-century colony.
A center of rebellion during
the drive for independence,
the town had deteriorated
when restoration began in the
1920s—an unprecedented
combination of vision and
scholarship and the patronage
of John D. Rockefeller, Jr. The
effort has rebuilt or restored
more than a hundred major
buildings, including King's Arms
Tavern (right) and Chowning's
Tavern (above), at a cost of 90
million dollars. The example of
Williamsburg inspired
preservationists across the land;
their efforts have grown to
today's nationwide phenomena,
encompassing the revival of
crafts, musical forms, antique
machines, ships and the ports
that sheltered them, gardens,
and entire communities.*

Modern Skills
Maintain Old Designs

was chartered to provide leadership and to encourage public participation. And in 1966 a new law authorized the establishment in the Department of the Interior of the National Register of Historic Places. It lists sites, districts, objects, and structures of significance in history, architecture, archaeology, engineering, and culture. In less than two decades the list has grown to more than 27,000 strikingly varied entries—Pony Express stables in Missouri, a convent in Puerto Rico, Thomas Jefferson's Monticello, a totem pole in Alaska, a firehouse in Hawaii.

"You name it, we have it," says William Murtagh, who served as the first Keeper of the Register and is now a vice president of the National Trust. Murtagh, an architectural historian, abhors the needless destruction of any relic of value and welcomes additions to the list as a means of encouraging protection.

The entries in the Register may still enjoy a useful life. John Milner, a busy preservation architect of West Chester, Pennsylvania, surveyed the old railroad stations along Amtrak's northeast corridor, from Boston to Baltimore. Planners thought modern passenger needs would require major changes in the terminals. But Milner's team found the original designs so well planned that many needed no major revamping. Beyond that, says Milner, most of the buildings played a historic role in the development of transportation and deserve a place in the Register.

In the troubled 1970s, Americans once more looked backward "in search of an orderly past." Historian Michael Kammen saw a

"yearning for a golden age of homespun, and for a lost innocence." These were also the years of Bicentennial pride and of a growing respect for ethnic experience. The quest for roots was under way.

The 1980s have brought no letup, according to Charles H. P. Duell, a member of the board of the National Trust. "More and more, people feel that a sense of history is important in their lives," says Duell, "and surely preservation helps satisfy that need. America has come of age to the point where we are recognizing both the economic and the aesthetic appeal of saving the tangible evidence of our own American past."

A sense of history. High school students in northeastern Georgia roam the Appalachian highlands with cameras and tape recorders, probing the depths of living memory to document the culture that nurtured them. Self-sufficiency was a hallmark of that highland culture, so from their elders the youngsters record how to tan a hide, build a coffin, deliver a baby, gather wild food, and make pure corn whiskey by the light of mountain moonshine.

"The old-timers," notes one observer, "tell things to youngsters they wouldn't say to anybody else." The tales go into the quarterly *Foxfire,* and from there into books, TV, recordings, and Broadway. The idea has spread like wildfire. Hundreds of similar projects are under way, from Maine to Alaska and Hawaii—including a publication by Navajo students in New Mexico.

A one-room schoolhouse in Des Moines provides the setting in which Iowa children

Extending the lifetime of an urban landmark, architect John Milner, standing, goes over plans to restore dormer windows and install sheet metal gutters at the Philadelphia College of Art. Old maps and blueprints and archaeological probing at the site often guide such restorations.

Go-between for the past and the future, actress Joanna Featherstone delights children in New York City with poems and songs by black Americans. Daughter of a Baptist preacher who acted out his sermons, she uses new compositions as well as traditional stories handed down orally.

FOLLOWING PAGES: *Sounds of New Orleans jazz vibrate through the city of its birth, as old-time musicians get together at Preservation Hall.*

become pupils of a century ago. They draw buckets of drinking water, carry armloads of firewood for the potbellied stove, and clean chalk dust from blackboard rags by beating them on a rail fence. And study the reading, writing, and arithmetic of the 1870s.

At living re-creations of old farms across the nation, young people learn that bacon and eggs at the breakfast table didn't come from an easy trip to the supermarket, but from a more basic and time-consuming source: "First you raise a chicken and a hog. . . ."

Visitors watch old skills in action at restored gristmills as millers convert wheat into flour and corn into meal. Or they can watch as mules plod in a circle to power a mill that grinds sugarcane into sweet juice.

A vicarious journey back to lives of rural toil can be understood better by swinging a scythe in the motions of harvest, or by gripping a plow's wooden handles burnished smooth by years of labor. To touch an old artifact is to feel the pulse of history.

Time slows along a small-town Main Street restored to its turn-of-the-century look, where town business and local news revolved endlessly and dependably, like the ubiquitous red-and-white pole at the barbershop.

The spirit of place can be recaptured by strolling the streets of a preserved colonial or 19th-century neighborhood in an otherwise up-to-date city. Consider the spirit of such a place as Old Town, in Alexandria, Virginia, lying near the nation's capital, rich in associations with George Washington and Gen. Robert E. Lee. William Murtagh lives in Old Town, not because of its famous sons, but because of its scale and harmony.

"Who lived where, who did what where—that's nice to know and those are things you point out to visitors," says Murtagh. "But I live in Alexandria because it has some of the best architecture in the Washington area, and because of its convenience.

"Remember, the 18th century and a lot of the 19th were pedestrian oriented, so that the whole scale of the community relates to the human norm. Alexandria for me is a walking city; its scale is my scale."

The long, low rows of restored houses, the narrow streets, the umbrella of foliage, brick sidewalks, cobblestones, red, gray, changing textures, timeworn surfaces—"the whole thing orchestrates to give me a sense of identity and locality."

Long-ago journeys can be shared in fantasy with former generations: the awe of seeing a broad-bottomed paddle-wheeler churning away from a riverside dock, or of watching an old locomotive surge into a station, panting steam like a massive beast precariously contained by two slender strips of metal rail.

Who does not stop to watch a bright, shiny antique auto chug past, or stand amazed as a vintage biplane rumbles across a bumpy field to soar gracefully heavenward like a bird unbound? Preservation has given us the depth of a third dimension. Through it we can see and touch America's living past.

Among those who keep the past alive, perhaps the most manifest skill is craftsmanship; and that respect of skill is still handed down from generation to generation.

Buildings of the French Quarter in New Orleans are bedecked with lacy ironwork—grilles, balcony railings, fences, and gates. Theodore M. Pierre, Jr., is the grandson and great-grandson of blacksmiths. His father, a master brickmason, has helped restore many buildings and garden walls and walkways in

the old city. In keeping with the tradition, young Theodore has become an architect.

"With each new generation," said Theodore, as we strolled the old French Quarter, "comes a rediscovery of the pleasures of craftsmanship." He once asked his father what was most enjoyable about his trade. "The idea," replied the elder Pierre, "that I can take a pile of sand and a bunch of bricks and make something beautiful that never was there before. Make it happen—here it is!"

One mason takes that pleasure of skill one step further. Richard Hossman of Gray, Maine, reproduces old bricks by using old methods. He and his crew mold local clay in vintage brickmaking machines. The newest one dates from the 1880s.

Every six weeks or so Hossman fires an old-fashioned woodburning kiln. Controlling heat by varying the draft and the placement of bricks in the kiln, he determines colors in the final result. One firing can produce bricks that vary from black to a variety of reds and even pale orange. They match the surface irregularities and color in older brickwork. Builders use them for old houses and to construct compatible new buildings in historic areas.

Uneven colors in the old brick may be one reason why people took to painting their brick walls. Another, suggests architect John Milner, was to provide waterproofing for inferior brick. Painting, he adds, also served in keeping up with the Joneses. When stucco started coming into vogue in the 19th century, he says, a coat of paint could substitute for the stylish finish.

Milner is fascinated by early technology—how a clay deposit became a brick, or how stone was quarried and hewn, or how a tree was chopped and sawed and shaped into paneling and beams. Before the mid-1800s, Milner notes, clay was forced into brick molds by hand, producing brick with uneven corners and surface irregularities. Masons compensated with heavy mortar joints. Late in the century steam-powered machines pressed clay into molds under great pressure. The bricks came out smooth, uniformly shaped—allowing thinner mortar joints. The new technology changed the appearance of brick walls, says Milner. They now looked much more regular, much more refined.

"Falling forwards from a bicycle is by no means a difficult exploit," an English viscount once wrote. "Indeed, the difficulty is to avoid performing it." Falling forward is especially easy on the high-wheel bicycles Robert Gerling restores and rides. I met Bob in Madison, Indiana, where he is curator of the historic Lanier House, an imposing Greek Revival mansion with long green lawns that stretch down to the Ohio River.

As I watched, he gave one of his high-wheelers a gentle push on the mansion's circular drive and mounted it up the back with a sprightly step. He set off at a good pace, circled back, and dismounted with a jump before the bicycle came to a stop.

"High-wheelers were popular only for about ten years," said Bob. "Too many people were killed or seriously hurt riding them."

In the 1880s, American bicycle clubs lobbied for better roads and erected some of the first traffic signs, even though a stop sign often proved ineffective. Brakes usually failed their intended purpose going downhill. The rider sits as high as five feet up on a high-wheeler, near the center of gravity and, with

Grasshopper vane has looked down on Boston since 1742, when Peter Faneuil set it atop the new market and meeting hall. Faneuil Hall itself became a weather vane of public moods—voiced by rebels and leaders from Paul Revere to John F. Kennedy.

luck, stays there. In the old days, even on a level straightaway, many a rider hit a bump or a pothole only to be quickly catapulted much farther along the road than his vehicle.

Bob belongs to a club of bicycle collectors, the Wheelmen, with more than 600 members in 39 states. Members haunt antique stores and barns to find old bikes. They also restore bikes and meet annually for rallies and companionship. They wear uniforms much like those of the first bicycle clubs—even using a bugler to signal commands to mount or dismount, just as the old cycling groups did.

The British sometimes referred to the high-wheelers as penny-farthings, comparing the sizes of the front and back wheels to large and small British coins. Before the 1880s ended, bicycles with wheels of equal size and chain drive had evolved—the safety bikes—and the high-wheelers gave way.

Today they're still riding high, and wheelwomen and children join the menfolk in regaining the spirit of another era. Those late 1800s were years of great inventions, of dreams that wheels or wings would speed us across continents or lift us high above the earth. Wilbur and Orville Wright and Glenn H. Curtiss maintained cycle shops, yet they saw beyond improved and safer bikes.

The Wrights, according to their biographers, saw little practical use for the primitive horseless carriages of the 1890s—rattly, mulish things that often refused to move, and a terror to horses when they did. The Wright brothers dreamed of flying machines, experimented with airfoils rigged to a bicycle, and with gliders and wind tunnels. In 1903, at Kitty Hawk, North Carolina, they left the ground in mankind's first successful, controlled flight in a powered airplane.

Curtiss's quest for speed led him to mount an engine on a cycle and improve the concept until he could race at more than a hundred miles an hour. He, too, designed aircraft and competed with the Wrights during the pioneering years of aviation.

Those bicycle days of the late 1800s were also times when many fashionable Americans summered at the seashore. A reminder of that time still stands on the beach at Margate City, New Jersey. Lucy, as she is fondly named, is an elephant crafted of metal and wood, as tall as a six-story building. Built in 1881, she has been called New Jersey's first elephant joke.

In her early years prospective real estate buyers climbed into her body and made their way to her howdah to look out upon building lots along the waterfront. But by 1902, an English family used Lucy's body as a summer home and dumped ashes down her trunk. As years passed, an aging Lucy confronted salt spray, hurricanes, and disrespect. She suffered the slings of beer bottles and two arrows of outrageous vandals, catching one shot in the rump and another in a shoulder. By 1970 much of her tin skin had sloughed away, exposing her decaying wooden ribs. And Lucy's sturdy 500-pound toes had rotted into the sand. Local sentiment—plus state and federal grants—saved Lucy to stand proudly restored in a Margate City park.

Twentieth-century effigy buildings, often designed as outsize ads for products or companies they identify, may become an embarrassment as the quick-changing fashions in advertising go out of style. Yet, as in Lucy's case, nostalgia and preservation sentiment have saved many from the wrecking crew. A 1930s Shell Oil service station shaped like the company's seashell logo still stands in Winston-Salem, North Carolina. And a 15,000-pound milk bottle that began service as a dairy bar in 1933 in Taunton, Massachusetts, was salvaged and moved to Boston's waterfront to become a lunch stand.

Preservationist Chester H. Liebs writes, "It is the new species of structures, signs and symbols—the gas station, diner, airport, motel, illuminated sign—that we have trouble evaluating because not enough time has elapsed to view them in perspective."

Taste in architecture is constantly being re-evaluated. A building seen as embarrassingly outdated by one may be viewed as a charming relic in the eyes of another. Vehement beholders often come to verbal and, increasingly, legal blows.

In 1932 Congress weighed the fate of the elaborately adorned State, War, and Navy Building in Washington, D. C., which was begun during Grant's Presidency. Senator Reed Smoot declaimed, "I never saw so many gimcracks and spizzerinktums put upon any other building I ever saw in the world." In retort, Senator George Norris declared his respect for spizzerinktums—whatever they might be. That mansarded, pavilioned, and chimneyed building in the Second Empire style still sprawls beside the White House, providing office space for the President's staff.

In the decade of that debate a fashionable style was Art Deco. In Florida resorts it gleamed with shiny metal that reflected a rainbow of pastel hues. Now Art Deco faces similar scrutiny. A Florida developer embroiled in a battle against the preservation of Art Deco buildings in Miami Beach recently puzzled aloud how buildings less than half a century old could be historic.

When the debate is lost, something can be saved. Salvage companies specializing in old artifacts glean ornaments and furnishings from houses and commercial buildings about to be razed. The salvage shops are favorite haunts of restorers and decorators.

I visited a Midwest warehouse several stories tall that was filled with salvaged treasures of Americana. Rows of heavy balustrades and cornices lined the walls. Iron grates from old heating registers lay in stacks. A glass-topped gasoline pump, a traffic light, church pews, iron gates, a porcelain shower head with matching knobs, giant keys, tiny tiles—these delightful oddments all lay under the heavy gaze of winged gargoyles high on the wall and the furtive glance of marble maidens clutching modestly at scraps of lily-white garments. Stained-glass windows and panels of beveled glass caught the light and shone—jewels that once bedecked the dowagers of architecture.

To undertake a project, to discover the perfect crystal doorknob or a complete staircase from an appropriate period is a restorer's dream. I wondered often at this deep satisfaction preservationists find in their quests. I began to feel that in one way it is an intuitive understanding, a personal sorting out.

As I sat in an open window on a dark evening in Philadelphia, a chilly spring rain seemed to set the Society Hill area apart, to emphasize a sense of the old and separate place and obliterate the high-rises that tower near it. I sat in a small hotel built in the 1830s and now restored as the Society Hill Hotel. As I sat, I became aware of the layers of history in the small space around me. Even then, the city was celebrating its tricentennial.

NATHAN BENN

Once again the area became the "greene Country Towne" of 1682—William Penn's dream, part of his "holy experiment" of love and tolerance. Rain-swept trees glistened. Neon signs glowed, then darkened. Traffic noises on the street below faded with reverie. Horse-drawn carriages laden with tourists approached from two directions, hooves tattooing on damp streets. The animals whinnied a greeting in passing.

Two blocks to my right, Independence Hall stood bathed in light. A short distance to my left, tall sailing ships lay moored at Penn's Landing, where the Quaker idealist first stepped ashore. I could see fine Georgian houses of successful merchants and the later no-nonsense Federal facades of houses built when Philadelphia was the nation's capital.

Dockmen of the mid-1800s lived in the building where I sat. They labored at loading and unloading heavy cargo in far-ranging ships. I could imagine the evening sound of slow footsteps as weary men climbed narrow stairs to lie down in narrow rooms.

In the 1860s dutiful patriots rallied there to sign on as Union soldiers in the recruiting office that opened onto the street below. They must have shouted inspired slogans, battle cries of freedom. They must have been eager to defend the Union and march southward to fight against unspeakable Rebel notions.

After 1890 the neighborhood became a low-rent district surrounding a busy food distribution center. Society Hill evolved into a haven for poor European immigrants, one step away from the port of entry and, with fortune, one generation away from success.

Through the years, buildings deteriorated and were altered, but most of Society Hill remained standing. Though it has been called the most historic square mile in the nation, Society Hill became a shabby slum destined for destruction.

A great surge of enthusiasm for architectural preservation in the 1950s and '60s saved it. National Park Service historian David Dutcher commented, "It got its spark from federal and local programs, but the impetus of preservation here has been private."

In an old house on Pine Street, I saw the restoration process in action. Mrs. Ralph Lemmer led me into her long double parlor filled with graceful antiques and strewn with sunlight. Twin fireplaces commanded one wall. I listened to her recount the knocking down, ripping up, scraping off, and smoothing over; the frustration of seemingly insurmountable problems; and the thrill of discovery. Kindness and patience showed in her pleasant face. Reviving such an architectural relic must be an act of love and lifetime dedication, I concluded.

"My husband and I started restoring this house in 1963," she said. "And we're still working." It was built in 1834 by a merchant. At one time it served as nurses quarters for a hospital; when the Lemmers bought it, the house was uninhabitable. "There was great camaraderie down here among people who bought houses to restore," Mrs. Lemmer added. "We learned a lot by looking at old houses and found material by visiting places being torn down. I bought old floorboards of longleaf yellow pine. I found locks, a door, these mantels. When we began to clean and scrape, I found that eight mantels already in the house were actually black marble that had been painted over. And when we scraped grimy paint off some of the old hinges, we discovered they were silver-plated."

I followed her up winding stairs and down short courses of steps to many levels, through bedrooms and sitting rooms already attractively restored. On the third story, we entered back rooms with dingy walls and encrusted floors. "There, another marble mantel is under that paint and dirt," she pointed out. "Here, a drain leaked." Water had cascaded down the freshly painted wall of the hallway. Mrs. Lemmer didn't seem surprised at my question, "What will you do with your time when the restoration is finished?"

With a smile she answered promptly, "Why, start all over again."

One family, one structure, one house lovingly preserved. To become involved in such a project, to live in such a place, to belong in its rooms, is to be enwrapped in history. Yet when one family remains with one house from one generation to the next for some 250 years, that belonging becomes a living legacy assumed at birth as easily as a name.

Middleton Place fronts a long curve of the Ashley River not far from Charleston, South Carolina. Its history goes back to the 1600s; the Williams family acquired it in 1729, and Mary Williams and Henry Middleton received it as dowry upon their marriage in 1741. The plantation has never been deeded out of the family.

The tidal river once served as a waterway connecting great plantations to the city and its port and binding them together into a community. Travelers could choose the river or, as I did, the Ashley River Road. It is perhaps the oldest road in South Carolina, in use by the 1670s and tracing a riverside Indian trail centuries older still. It passes through a tunnel of live oaks grown so large and outspread that they interlace high overhead, often obliterating sky, gently sweeping the air with graceful trails of Spanish moss. On the brightest of days the old road generates a mood of timelessness, of enchantment.

In 1741, the year he was married and came into ownership, Henry Middleton began carving forests and marshy wilderness into formal gardens. The geometric design included terraced lawns, ornamental lakes, walkways, arbors, and bowling greens. There was a wide view of the river, as well as minor vistas at strategic viewpoints. It took nearly a decade to complete the gardens, and later generations added to them.

The famous French botanist André Michaux put in a botanical garden across the Ashley in the 1780s. He had come to the new nation—its struggle aided by France—seeking plants that could grow timber for French ships. But he also introduced plants here—mimosa, gingko, pomegranate. To his neighbors he brought four camellias, perhaps the first planted in an American garden. Three of these bushes still stand at Middleton Place.

Though rice was grown in swamps and along river marshes, Middleton Place was not primarily an agricultural estate; it served as the family seat for other flourishing plantations. It survived British occupation during the Revolution, but Union troops set fire to the house in 1865. An earthquake in 1886 toppled the ruins. Only the gutted south wing survived. The owners, impoverished by the war, could no longer maintain the estate. The artificial lakes dried up and the gardens, so painstakingly nurtured, grew wild.

In 1915 Henry Middleton's great-great-great-grandson, J. J. Pringle Smith, announced to his young wife, "Calm yourself—I have inherited a 'white elephant', a seven thousand acre estate and nothing to maintain it with." But they moved there with their young daughter and began restoration. Mrs. Smith later wrote a journal for her grandchildren—"to give them some idea of Middleton Place since I have lived there."

In it she recalled the excitement of "finding the most inexpensive chintz—15 cents a yard—with a pattern of pink azaleas in a shop in Charleston and making the bedrooms gay and fresh." The family adjusted to a pinched life-style of "kerosene lamps. . . . no fresh milk . . . as we couldn't afford a cow. No bathrooms and no water in the house. Open fireplaces, making warm rooms impossible. Living seventeen miles from any source of supply—over incredibly bad roads, having a T-model which I couldn't drive. No telephone, no mail service. It is difficult now to believe how we carried on and survived the obstacles as they came."

Mrs. Smith described the gardens as overgrown with tangled honeysuckle, smilax, and bramble. Yellow jasmine completely covered the camellia bushes.

I strolled the restored gardens with the Smiths' grandson, Charles H. P. Duell, the present owner. He bears a resemblance to some Middleton family portraits of handsome, dark-haired men.

"I remember as a child being here often with my grandmother," he began. "I didn't realize it at the time, but I was absorbing influences. I remember her telling me that when they moved here many of the paths were overgrown. She had to get down on her hands and knees to feel the bricks that lined them to know just where they went. They fell into a geometric pattern. She knew things would be symmetrical and balanced."

We stopped to look down long, camellia-bordered walkways—allées in the language of formal gardens. The camellias, as tall as small trees, had passed their peak of bloom. Limbs of the glossy sentinels strewed red, white, and pink petals across the pale pathways. We wandered past wide, terraced lawns that stretched down toward the river, their shapes accented by the golden light of late afternoon. The poet Amy Lowell wrote of them: "Step lightly down these terraces, they are records of a dream."

Charles told me of another who walked the gardens. "There was a ghost, the Little Gray Lady. She appeared from the time the house was burned during the Civil War until the 1920s," he said. "Workers living here described seeing her frequently at twilight moving through the ruins." Then, after the restoration was well under way, she was seen no more. One of the older workers knew why: "She won't walk no more in the garden," he declared. "You see, the garden is cared for now." Preservationists know that good stewardship is needed for the proper care of property. Perhaps, said Charles, the Little Gray Lady was trying to provide a bit of stewardship during the long decades of neglect.

To visitors, Middleton Place is a living environment of the 18th- and 19th-century plantation. Sheep are shorn and their wool is spun, then dyed with plant dyes and woven. Lean, scruffy, long-bristled hogs are raised to resemble their ill-bred ancestry of razorbacks, or "pineland rooters," that foraged the woodland floor. Horses, cows, ducks, chickens wander the stableyard. The potter at the kick wheel, the blacksmith at his forge, the carpenter with his antique tools—Middleton Place is bustling again.

As plantations once flourished or slipped into decay, so did the city of Charleston, for they were tied by ownership and economy. Like Middleton Place, the port city saw its elegance fade with the gloom of the Civil War.

Blight and neglect gnawed at Charleston until early in this century. Then Susan Pringle Frost, remembered as a little old white-haired lady of distinguished family, set about to save what she could of the city. In 1920 she and a group of concerned citizens founded the city's first preservation society, and in 1931 part of old Charleston became the first historic district in the nation through enactment of a city ordinance.

The effect of that ordinance, observes architectural historian William Murtagh, was to extend the police powers of government—to a level then unknown—to control what a private citizen could do with his own property. It went beyond ordinary land-use zoning. In the interest of preservation it could limit an owner's choice of paint colors to those documented for the period.

Since Charleston's pioneering example, historic districts have been created throughout the nation. And in 1976 new tax policies encouraged efforts to save historic sites. Financially, it could now be more attractive to reuse an old income-producing building than to destroy it and build anew. With the promise of profit, preservation activity surged. And even with new tax-law modifications in the 1980s, solid incentives still exist.

But preservation often must deal with progress. Cities and suburbs and road networks expand. All this may require compromise. And what is lost is mourned.

Thousands of visitors each year demonstrate the value of preserving Middleton Place. Its gardens have been called "in effect an organic historical document." The botanical gardens of André Michaux once grew a few miles away. He had botanized in Europe and the Orient and in America from Florida to Canada, collecting many species new to science. Five flowering plant species of the Carolinas honor his name. Today the Michaux gardens near Charleston are gone.

Changing attitudes have spawned new types of archaeology—urban, commercial, industrial—giving fresh insights into recent history. The more complete the relic from the past, the more complete the understanding in the present. In that sense, preservationists practice what may be called preventive archaeology, by conserving the tangible, living record of American experience.

Perhaps it is a kind of human imperative to preserve the past. It may serve to assuage our fears and insecurities in spanning our lives from birth, through dynamic changes, to death. It places us in time.

Recently I sat with my daughter on the front porch of her rented farmhouse in North Carolina. A vibrant summer sunset and a whippoorwill's song peacefully closed the day.

"You know," I said, "some of our family had land in this county until the Revolution, but they moved south. They were on the winning side, not like our family in the Civil War." She gazed across the rolling pastures to a dense forest.

"What if this were their land," she mused. "Too bad we can't reclaim it."

But in spirit We already had.

From Untamed Land to

Farmer rasps a hoof at the Colonial Pennsylvania Plantation, a working farm west of Philadelphia,

Fertile Fields

By H. Robert Morrison
Photographs by Annie Griffiths

with tools and techniques from days when Redcoats and Patriots fought over this land.

The stone ax bit cleanly into the sapling. Chips flew and the flaked edge of the ancient tool severed the branch as quickly and cleanly as a sharp steel hatchet. The man continued working in silence, using the same versatile stone tool. One edge chopped; another edge, serrated, worked like a fine-tooth saw. A rounded notch shaved off curls of bark in neat strips, planing the branch smooth.

The man was John White, part Cherokee and an anthropologist with the Kampsville Archaeological Center, in Illinois. He has learned an astonishing range of Stone Age skills, from foraging the countryside for wild foods to chipping stone arrowheads and spear points. Watching John work made it easy to picture the world he sought to re-create, the world of the hunters and gatherers who once occupied this land.

Within half an hour the work was finished: a smooth stick about a foot long with an inch-deep slot cut in one end. Holding it up, John asked if anyone knew what it was.

"A spear?" ventured one of the schoolchildren seated around him. "Almost right," John replied. Reaching into his pocket, he pulled out a stone point and inserted it into the slot. The stone fitted precisely, staying in place even without the binding of sinew the ancient hunters would have used.

John now had the business end, or foreshaft, of a spear. It would fit into the socket of a longer shaft to form the complete hunting weapon. Why a two-piece spear? The longer shaft, John explained, had to be very smooth,

strong, and well balanced for throwing. Since it was harder to make, the longer piece was more valuable; and by making it detachable the hunter could save it even if several of the shorter pieces were broken or carried off by wounded prey.

In such fashion, guided by clues dug from the earth, John White revives the skills and strategies with which early Americans confronted the land. I had sought him out in a quest for America's rural past—a journey that led me from Pennsylvania's woodlands to California's Napa Valley, from lush Iowa cornfields to the arid mesas of the Hopi tribal lands in Arizona.

On working farms and in ceremonies steeped in tradition, I discovered how men and women honored and preserved the ways of their ancestors—the world of Indian people, of colonial farmers, of sodbusters and settlers and mountain folk.

This day at Kampsville had begun with a group of schoolchildren gathered in an oval-shaped, high-domed wigwam that John had built with stone tools, a dwelling like those the Woodland Indians had known. John had driven saplings into the ground, bent the tops inward to form the roof, lashed them with strips of bark and cordage of plant fibers, and covered them with mats woven of reeds.

A small fire flickered on the hearth near the center of the floor where John sat. We reclined on platforms built high enough to provide storage space underneath yet low enough so that we were below the smoke filtering upward. Under John's spell, in the

Aprons bulge with corn sown, hoed, and picked in the pioneer manner at Living History Farms at Des Moines, Iowa. Here unfolds the story of Iowa farming—in changing houses, livestock, cookery, and technology—from settler struggles to the rich promise of 1900.

gloom of the cozy interior, the village became our home. It was late autumn; the game had moved off and the hunters would follow. But the snows and ice of winter might make hunting all but impossible. We would have to depend on the dried corn hanging from the rafters. Scarce game and a harsh winter would bring suffering to the village.

Later, as darkness crept over the village, John told me why keeping the ancient crafts alive was important to him.

"The values and skills of the past are our legacy," he said. "They belong to the future as well. In a very real sense I'm doing this for the generations to come, that they will gain respect and understanding for all our ancestors." Fellow anthropologists, students—including, at times, Indians—visit the Kampsville Archaeological Center to understand the life of an earlier America.

Some of the legacy that John White respects comes not from archaeology or scholarly treatises but directly from his Cherokee forebears—reflecting an interest that is widely shared by other native Americans. Among the most devoted in the pursuit of this interest are the Hopi people of northeastern Arizona. There the Hopis have lived for centuries in naturally fortified villages, on three mesas that rise above the flat desert like the prows of sandbound ships.

One of the most important means of preserving ancestral traditions, of maintaining "the Hopi Way," has been through ancient farming rituals. These have been handed down for countless generations until often their rationale has been forgotten, and only the ways themselves survive.

One afternoon I joined Terrance Talaswaima, his 11-year-old son Terry, Jr., and his father in the family cornfield. By Hopi custom the fields are allotted through the wife's family group. In that sense, the field belongs to her, although the planting and cultivation are the husband's responsibility.

While his father and son chopped at a few scraggly weeds, Terry pointed out a number of traditions embodied in the field. The corn was planted in rows of hills. None of the rows ran straight across the field; after a certain number of hills, the row ended and another row, slightly offset from the first, began. When I asked Terry why, he shrugged. That it had always been done that way was reason enough. He had learned the ancient ways much as his son was now learning, absorbing traditions as part of everyday life.

Near the center of the field stood the prayer shrine, a bower of evergreen branches about a foot high. From the branches fluttered prayer feathers. The Hopi people believe that these soft white eagle feathers carry messages from this world to the spiritual one.

The corn rose green and sturdy; though fully grown, it stood only waist-high. As Terry pushed aside the leaves, I could see that each stalk bore three or four good-size ears. An ancient strain, Hopi corn can be planted as deep as a foot and a half to take advantage of subsurface moisture. It sends roots down several feet, and its short stalk exposes less area to the hot sun and drying winds. Most corn planted today is yellow, red, white, or blue—colors that have special sacred significance to Terry's people.

"The earth spirit gave the Hopis corn when we entered this world long ago," Terry told me. "Ever since, corn has been important to the Hopi people. A Hopi infant is given an ear of corn at birth, and this is called your 'corn

FOLLOWING PAGES: *Neatly clad plowman, whip in hand, drives his team of oxen to break the sod at Old Sturbridge Village, Massachusetts, a museum community that pursues the rounds of rural life of the early 1800s. This breaker plow with its steel share helped westering farmers turn heavy prairie soils. In New England, plowmen more typically used iron shares—forged and, later, cast. With the 1900s motor tractors clattered into the fields and revolutionized agriculture.*

mother'—your spiritual mother. It symbolizes the strength that will be with you throughout your lifetime.

"Every major ceremony requires that you have an ear of corn with you, as your spiritual identity. At your death corn is prepared, to sustain you as you enter the spiritual world.

"From planting to harvest," Terry concluded, "the corn belongs to the man. After harvest it is the woman's. She is responsible for preserving the seed corn for planting, as well as preparing the corn for eating."

In the village of Shongopovi on Second Mesa, Alice Kabotie, a dignified woman with graying hair, showed me how the Hopis prepare the rolled cornmeal bread called *piki*. Mrs. Kabotie sat in her small piki house, made of concrete blocks and set a few steps from her kitchen. Under her piki stone burned a fire of dry juniper wood. Beside her, a pottery bowl held a thin batter of blue cornmeal mixed with water and ashes.

Dipping her hand into the bowl, Mrs. Kabotie swept it across the flat, hot stone, leaving a thin film. Several more times she repeated the smooth, swift motion until the surface was covered. When the edges started to curl, she lifted the sheet and covered the stone with more of the batter.

It was hot, exacting work, made more difficult by the necessity of continuing without interruption so the stone could be kept at the proper temperature. When Mrs. Kabotie finished, she offered me one of the rolls of piki with a smile. Its blue-gray layers, so tissue-thin they were translucent, were as delicate as their light corn flavor.

Just as religion permeates every aspect of Hopi life, so the significance and symbolism of corn extend throughout Hopi religious activities. Piki and other traditional corn dishes accompany religious dances and ceremonies. Combined with their conservatism, their dedication to the Hopi Way, and their isolated location, the Hopis' centuries-old techniques of dry farming and food preparation have greatly contributed to the enduring vitality of their cultural heritage.

Unlike the Hopi, whose system of agriculture had evolved within North America, the early European settlers in the colonies brought with them the farming techniques they had learned in their native lands.

Across a low wooden bridge over Ridley Creek, in a state park 15 miles west of Philadelphia, I entered another century. In a pasture bounded by a split-rail, zigzagging worm fence, a horned red Devon cow chewed her cud. Smoke rose from the kitchen chimney of the stone farmhouse roofed with wooden shingles; inside, bread lay baking on the hearth. In a cleared field beside the house, a farmer wearing breeches and waistcoat urged along his team of horses as they dragged a handmade wooden harrow to ready the ground for planting. A barefoot boy tipped a wooden bucket of kitchen scraps into a muddy pen where pigs grunted and rooted.

The centuries had been turned back by the Colonial Pennsylvania Plantation. Here volunteers and staff members pursue the daily rounds of a farmstead of Revolutionary days and welcome visitors from the 20th century on summer weekends.

Some colonists regarded the year 1777 with foreboding; its numerals reminded them of the shape of a gallows. Yet the Americans gained several (Continued on page 48)

Skills of
the Stone Age

Lessons in an outdoor classroom introduce students to techniques of Stone Age toolmakers. Anthropologist John White, of the Kampsville Archaeological Center, in western Illinois, coaches the potters, shaping clay dug from creek banks. With hands and teeth he twists strands of basswood bark into two-ply cord. To make a spear foreshaft, he notches a stick with a stone flake (top right), carefully flexes the stick against his knee to make the wood fibers break just right, inserts a stone spearpoint into the slotted end, and lashes it tight. The new foreshaft (lower right) resembles an ancient one found in a cave.

Maize Flavors
Hopi Culture

Her breath a winnowing breeze, a Hopi woman in Arizona bounces kernels to separate the chaff as she prepares hominy for stew. Hand shelling (below) had popped the kernels from the ears. A batter of corn, water, and ash (opposite) makes piki *bread. Spread tissue thin, the batter sizzles on a hot griddle, or piki stone. Hopi people use piki both as food and for spiritual sustenance—in religious rites that celebrate the venerable bonds between the Hopi and earth's gift of maize.*

FOLLOWING PAGES: *Young dancer slips into a ceremonial room, or kiva, during corn-harvest rites at San Ildefonso Pueblo in New Mexico. Evergreens, seashells, and furs signify close spiritual ties to nature.*

ALL BY TERRY EILER

42

Riding the Cowboy Trail

Lore of the Old West lingers in the Great Basin country of southeast Oregon, a domain of cattle barons. A cowhand lassoes a calf, and Ed Davis, operator of the 250,000-acre Alvord Ranch, helps with the branding (opposite)—traditional chores of the western range that live on today. Cowpoke canines have long helped with herding; here a ranch dog hems in a rambunctious yearling.

Trail drives, in these days of cattle trucks, have gone the way of the Pony Express. But for old times' sake—and for the fun of it—the Alvord bunch may drive the critters 60 miles from winter to summer range.

victories earlier that year. Then the British, campaigning toward the Patriot capital of Philadelphia, tricked George Washington into a tactical blunder at Brandywine Creek. The diary of Benjamin Hawley, a farmer who lived near Ridley Creek, reveals how one colonist reacted to the momentous events taking place around him.

On September 11, the day of the battle, Hawley wrote: "Very hot; finished harrowing the rye; the English Engaged the Americans, the latter defeated with much loss." The next day: "Cloudy; putting up fences that the American Soldiers [broke] in their retreat." The War of Independence rated a mention, but Hawley's first concern was his property.

It was a nonpartisan concern, as witness the entry of September 13: "Some of ye English Soldiers had Sundries to ye value of 8 shillings and did not pay."

Other than salting, smoking, pickling, and drying, 18th-century families had few ways of preserving food. Milk, even when stored in the cool stream in the stone springhouse, would keep at most for a week. Made into cheese, however, it could remain edible much longer. Anne Vince, a sturdy woman in a white cap, chemise, and an ankle-length skirt, stood barefoot in the porch of the springhouse, stirring a pot of sour milk hung over a wood fire. Her very speech, with more than a trace of her native England remaining, lent authenticity to the scene.

When the milk had warmed, Anne added rennet, with its milk-curdling enzyme, and strained off the liquid whey through cheesecloth. The last step was squeezing the curds as dry as possible in a wooden cheese press, made at the plantation to an 18th-century pattern. The prepared rennet, however, is a

modern touch. Colonial housewives used the membrane of a calf's stomach to provide the curdling enzyme.

"Try this other cheese," Anne invited. "It's only a few days old, but it will give you an idea of the taste." She cut a sliver of the soft cheese for me. It crumbled and melted on my tongue, and its sharp, salty tang gave promise of very good eating.

The springhouse itself preserved all manner of perishables—in all seasons. Its spring, with median temperatures between 50° and 56°F, retards spoilage in summer and prevents freezing in winter.

At the pigsty, farm manager Terry Mank told me about his backbreeding program. From descriptions that have been found, he said, typical pigs of the 18th century did not look much like those farmers raise today. The earlier pigs looked wilder, rangier, leaner, with longer noses. "We're selectively breeding pigs to bring back those characteristics," Terry added. "Most farmers want to improve their stock. Here at the plantation, we're doing just the opposite. We're trying to breed the wildness back into these animals."

Meat and produce, fencing and furniture, tools and firewood, wool and linen for clothing—all these produced by farmers of the 1700s made them largely self-sufficient. However, grinding grain by hand was extremely tiring and time-consuming, so they turned to a local specialist, the miller, to have their grain ground into flour.

On Nantucket Island off the Massachusetts coast an 18th-century mill remains standing, one of a few such mills still working by wind power alone. "The first mill on the island was built in 1666," miller John A. Stackpole told me, adding with a chuckle: "This one wasn't built until comparatively recently—1746." As the four 30-foot-long vanes turned gracefully in the breeze, wooden-toothed gears and spinning granite millstones rumbled a rhythmic growl inside.

With his fringe of neatly trimmed white beard, Stackpole looked the part of a sea captain, as his Nantucket ancestors were.

"A Nantucket sailor named Nathan Wilbur had seen windmills in England and Holland," the miller said, "and he decided that Nantucket, with its steady winds, would be an ideal location for a windmill. He didn't get much support from his neighbors, and so he built it himself, using his knowledge of ship carpentry and the design he had observed in windmills abroad."

We climbed the steep, narrow stairway to the mill's second level, where a two-ton millstone turned against a stationary nether stone. Corn dribbled from a wooden hopper into the hole at the center of the moving stone. Ground into flour, it moved outward off the edge and fell down a chute to the sifter on the lower level, where coarse grits were separated from fine flour.

"The flow of corn needs careful adjustment," John noted. "Too much, and it's not ground fine enough. Too little, and the stones can overheat and damage the corn."

Owned by the Nantucket Historical Association since 1897, the mill has escaped the fates of its neighbor mills: One of them was blown up in 1837; lightning destroyed another; the third was pulled down for its lumber.

This one very nearly came to a similar end. "Jared Gardner bought it for firewood in 1828 for $20," said John, "but when the canny Quaker inspected his purchase, he found it could be repaired. Gardner did the work

himself and sold the mill for a good profit.

"You know, in the old days the miller was an important man in the community. Often farmers would wait while their grain was ground, exchanging news and gossip with the miller. In a way my job here is something like that. All summer I get to meet visitors from all over the world."

By 1840, Nantucket was well established as a prosperous whaling center. Philadelphia had become a city of 93,000 people. The frontier had pushed westward to the prairies.

On the frontier the rolling grasslands stretched to the horizon. Streams wound through fringes of woodland. Indians hunted across the prairie terrain, but few of them lived there permanently. Grass so tall it would hide a man on horseback awed the early settlers. At first they spurned the land; if it wouldn't grow trees, it must not be good for farming. But a handful of pioneers found that strong, vigorous crops sprang from the black earth.

Within a year after the Black Hawk War ended in 1832, the Iowa prairies were open to settlement and attracted thousands. A very few were the loners, men who picked up and moved when they could hear the ring of a neighbor's ax. Most were seeking security in land—in good farmland and a bit of woodland for building a cabin and for firewood.

For a time the land resisted. The virgin turf grew so thick in many places that a team could not pull a wooden plow through it. Some settlers planted anyhow, poking holes into the grasslands and dropping seeds. Others hired itinerant sodbusters whose giant steel plows, pulled by three to eight yokes of

Colonial Farm Life:
Homemade and Handhewn

oxen, cut a furrow two feet wide. By 1850, Iowa's population numbered nearly 200,000.

On rolling countryside at the western edge of Des Moines stands a graphic reminder of those pioneer days. It is one part of Living History Farms, a private foundation that, as the name suggests, operates farms depicting the changes in rural life on the Iowa prairie—from the early days of settlement to the beginning of the 20th century.

"Just about everything was done by hand on farms like this one," Dave Miles, manager of the foundation's Pioneer Farm, told me. "The farmer who had horses was the fortunate one. The rest hitched up their cows for plowing, and for the other work used their own muscle power. It was a hard life, at first. The crops and vegetables they grew, the fish they caught, and the game they hunted fed the family; there wasn't much left over for trade."

Built by hand using broadaxes, adzes, and other tools of the 1840s, the pioneer cabin is authentic in virtually every detail. During my visit a quilting frame stood in the dooryard near a smoke-blackened kettle used earlier that day for making soap. On a cabin wall near the plank door ears of corn, their husks pulled back and braided together, had been hung to dry.

"Hello, come on in and visit for a while," called a voice from the cabin. Inside, it took a moment for my eyes to adjust to the gloom. Elaine Hargenrader stood at the rough table, shaping biscuits and placing them in a Dutch oven; Mary Schmidt sat in a rocker, shelling beans into an earthenware bowl.

A double bed built into a corner dominated the cabin's single room. From a covered kettle in the fireplace came the mouth-watering aroma of the ham the people of the farm would eat at noon.

Elaine covered the cast-iron Dutch oven, set it at the edge of the fireplace, and heaped glowing embers on its lid. This modest utensil served pioneer women as their oven—the only means they had of baking.

"We've been able to find which vegetables pioneers grew in Iowa," Elaine said as she showed me the kitchen garden, "and we've planted the same varieties here. We've found, for example, that some varieties of beans gave much higher yields than others, and yet the pioneers continued to plant several lower-yielding types. We're now trying to find out why. Maybe some of them kept better through the winter, or were more resistant to drought, insects, or blight."

About the same time that the pioneers in Iowa were building cabins and breaking the prairie sod, California pioneer growers were planting winemaking varieties of grapes. Their efforts expanded dramatically after the gold rush of 1849 brought thousands of thirsty newcomers to the West Coast.

Jacob Schram, a German barber, established the first hillside winery in the Napa Valley northeast of San Francisco near the hot-springs town of Calistoga in the 1860s. Initially, to support his family, he continued his trade, riding among the ranches to slicken up their proprietors. By 1880, when author Robert Louis Stevenson (Continued on page 57)

Barefoot milkmaid—in the footsteps of 18th-century Quakers—skims curds of cheese from a pot of whey at the Colonial Pennsylvania Plantation. Farm wives in the 1700s stored such perishables in a springhouse, where cool, seeping water provided free refrigeration.

Splashing across Ridley Creek, a mare in 18th-century harness drags a tree for firewood at the colonial plantation. Two centuries ago the fire might burn constantly for cooking and heating—20 cords of wood a year cut, dragged, sawed, split, *and stacked. Sawyers then worked mainly with English blades; later, logging brought forth the American-made perforated lance-tooth saw— designed to avoid clogging. One of them (opposite) bucks a log in Pennsylvania.*

FOLLOWING PAGES: *Life seems cozy for the porker at Iowa's Living History Farms—a neat pen, women bringing corn. But in pioneer days the pigpen meant that the season of running wild had ended as wintertime butchering drew nigh.*

visited Schramsberg Vineyards, Schram himself was a prosperous proprietor. Gangs of laborers had dug extensive cellars into the hillside, cool caverns where thousands of bottles of wine lay maturing.

"The stirring sunlight, and the growing vines, and the vats and bottles in the cavern, made a pleasant music for the mind," wrote Stevenson. I retraced the Scottish author's steps and enjoyed the same pleasant music.

"When I first walked onto this property in 1965," Jack Davies, the current proprietor, told me, "the winery was a dormant, ghostlike place. The vineyards were overgrown with trees, manzanita shrubs, and poison oak. It was a jungle."

Schramsberg had become a casualty of Prohibition; this national experiment of the early 20th century had closed all the wineries except those few licensed to produce sacramental and medicinal wines. Surprisingly, grape production actually increased during those years. Some grapes, instead of being pressed into wine, were dried and pressed into cakes—many of them labeled with the warning that if they were mixed with sugar and water and allowed to ferment, the result would be an illegal beverage.

Jack Davies restored the house and cellars at Schramsberg, and cleared and replanted the vineyard. Like other vintners of Napa Valley, today a world-famed wine center, Davies does not hesitate to use modern laborsaving machines and winemaking techniques. But even today, Robert Louis Stevenson would recognize the place he visited a century ago.

"Why did you restore an old winery," I asked Davies, "instead of starting out anew?"

He thought a moment before replying.

"I have a feeling that there's something inside human beings that prompts a respect, an interest, an appreciation for traditions and heritage," he said. "I thought it would be exciting if I could take an old, abandoned business and make it into a useful, productive center of activity."

Schramsberg is one of many Napa Valley vineyards brought back to life. On a mountainside west of St. Helena, Greg Bissonette pointed out one of the original stained-glass windows set into the three-foot-thick stone wall of Chateau Chevalier. Modeled after a French chateau, it was built by George Chevalier, the son of a French stained-glass craftsman who had made his fortune as a spirits merchant in San Francisco. Along with the name, the date "1891" glowed in the window.

"I wanted to use that lovely old window as the design for my wine label," said Greg. "But all labels have to be approved by the federal government. When I submitted mine, they required me to add the words 'Established 1891' to explain the date in the design. They didn't want anyone to think that 1891 was the vintage of the wine inside the bottles!"

With some difficulty Greg and his family have put grapes back on the steep hillsides originally cultivated by Chevalier. Early growers had planted the vines on the slopes as the most practical way of limiting frost damage.

Out of the 1870s with his sleeve garters and felt derby, Art Dickey smiles in the customers and visiting "jawsmiths" at the Walnut Hill general store in Iowa. Technology of the era lined the shelves with factory-made hardware and other products that eased the drudgery of farm life.

With mechanization most vineyards moved downhill. Then, as California winemaking soared, grapevines have climbed uphill.

Across the Napa Valley, east of Yountville, stands another building completed about the same time as Chateau Chevalier. High above it looms the ridge said to have been named Stags' Leap by the builder, Chicago financier Horace Chase. In the 1920s the grand three-story home was turned into a hotel. Carl and Joanne Doumani bought the property in 1970 and began restoring the vineyards and buildings of Stags' Leap Winery.

Palms surround the gray stone house; a shady and inviting veranda sweeps around two sides. At one corner rises a round stone turret. From the gutters rain runs down along lengths of heavy chain, rather than through downspouts. It is still a grand old house, but today it stands only two stories high.

"The top story was a total loss," Joanne told me over tea in their airy, high-ceilinged living room. "We had to tear it off, and then we began restoration. Looking back, it seemed like a hundred years war."

With evident pride Joanne showed me through, pausing to point out the fine red-wood fireplace mantel and recalling the seemingly endless tasks of tearing out crumbling plaster, refinishing soot-blackened woodwork, and restoring intricately coffered, 14-foot-high ceilings.

In that same vibrant decade of the 1840s—when vineyards took root in northern California, Iowa settlers turned the prairie sod, and the United States pushed its boundaries to the Pacific—an immigrant community planted its hopes and its culture in south-central Texas. The community and its culture survived the pioneer challenge; both live on, amid prosperous farms and ranches between San Antonio and Johnson City.

New Braunfels is German, and proud of it. It was founded in 1845 by Prince Carl of Solms-Braunfels, who had been appointed to search for land in Texas where German immigrants could settle. An *Adelsverein*—association of noblemen—seeking to ease the pressures of overpopulation and hoping to make a profit from land sales, had formed the Society for the Protection of German Immigrants in Texas to promote emigration. Many of the newcomers had been tradesmen and intellectuals in the old country, and they found themselves poorly equipped for the frontier. Yet they struggled on.

Their efforts paid off. Frederick Law Olmsted, a young New England journalist who would later gain fame as the designer of New York's Central Park, visited New Braunfels some eight years after its founding. "I do not know a prettier picture of contented prosperity," he observed. He also noted a type of house "having exterior plaster-work, or brick, laid up between the timbers." The style resembled Tudor half-timbered houses; it had come from central Germany, where it was called *Fachwerk*. A surprising number of these homes still stand in New Braunfels, and fachwerk is a commonly heard word.

One of the houses was built in 1852 by Carl Friedrich Baetge, a civil engineer who had earlier built a railroad in Russia. In its time his fachwerk home was the grandest in the county. In 1970 the New Braunfels Conservation Society dismantled the old house at its original rural site and had the timbers hauled into the town to Conservation Plaza, which is devoted to the area's historic architecture. Years went by; Baetge House faced an uncertain future.

"I just couldn't stand to see the framework of that fine old home lying out in the weather," middle school history teacher Barron Schlameus told me as we sat in the dining room of the restored house. He had already rehabilitated three rundown fachwerk structures and joined them together to make a home for himself, but transforming that pile of timbers into a standing house was more than one man could handle. Students volunteered summer vacation time, working at minimum wages. The result is a handsome fachwerk museum house.

Where did the money come from? Mostly from the conservation society, said Schlameus. At the start, important help also came from the Wurstfest.

Inside a cavernous building—once a warehouse—on the festival grounds, thousands of visitors ate sausage and sauerkraut, washing them down with foaming mugs of beer. Oompah music filled the hall; young and old crowded the dance floor.

"But Wurstfest is more than polkas and beer," J. C. Reagan reminded me. A lawyer with a neatly trimmed mustache and an infectious smile, Reagan was serving as president of the Wurstfest Association, Inc. "We discovered early on that we weren't just selling sausage. We were promoting the German heritage of New Braunfels."

When I visited the Heritage Exhibit, held annually during the Wurstfest, hostess Betty Reinarz told me that "local people not only volunteer their time and effort to plan and build these exhibits; they also bring out their own antiques and family heirlooms—things

the public would otherwise never have a chance to see." One scene portrayed the wedding of Olinska Sippel and William Robert Posey on October 28, 1902. The room was decorated as it had been described in a newspaper article about the wedding; the bride mannequin wore the actual 1902 beaded wedding dress; and the groom's brocaded vest and stiff collar were likewise the real thing.

The heritage displays ranged from a traditional German Christmas scene to a parlor funeral—popular among the visiting schoolchildren—and, of course, included a demonstration of old-time sausage making.

New Braunfels is one of many places where teenage energy and curiosity have enhanced efforts to preserve local history. In Missouri I watched one group at work—high school students of Lebanon who record Ozark lifeways and crafts of earlier days in the pages of *Bittersweet* magazine.

The student staff members, said faculty adviser Ellen Gray Massey, not only produce the magazine but also run the business. The memories of Ozark elders provide much of the editorial input. One afternoon, with assistant adviser Delilah Shotts, I sat in while reporters Lisa Mestan, Terri Heck, and Lisa Goss, glowing in their youth, found out how farm women raised babies half a century and more ago. Lorene Amos, Flora Lamkins, and Mary Jane Hough, ranging in age from 73 to 87, remembered.

They remembered that babies wore a white band around their bodies for the first six weeks to keep the navel from protruding. Infants of 70 or 80 years ago also wore long gowns with the excess length folded back against the body. When a baby began to toddle, the gown was cut to ankle length. The

Traditions Ripen on California Vines

piece cut off, stitched to a yoke, made another gown. Nothing went to waste.

Baby clothes were scrubbed with lye soap, boiled, and rinsed. Tedious work, the reporters noted. True, said the women, which is why they didn't always wash diapers that were merely wet, but just hung them in the sun.

The chores seemed endless, and in those days Mother didn't expect—or get—housekeeping help from Father. How did busy mothers keep young ones out of the way? Store-bought toys were few, but there were homemade blocks and rag dolls, and pictures in the Sears, Roebuck catalog. Or the baby might be offered a feather with molasses on it; the feather would stick to one tiny hand, then the other, and back and forth. When baby's hands were busy, Mother's hands were free—for a little while.

One autumn morning I stepped inside the one-room schoolhouse at Walnut Hill, the 1870s-era town at Living History Farms in Iowa. Boys and girls bent over their slates as the teacher, her dark hair pulled back into a bun, offered advice and encouragement. Fifth graders from a Des Moines school were learning history here by living it.

The students had completed their exercises in penmanship—up-and-down straight strokes and oval curlicues. Now they were copying the maxim from the blackboard: "Silence is golden." The only sounds were of chalk whispering against slate.

For one left-handed youngster the exercise was especially difficult. In the schools of the 1870s, explained the teacher, *every* student had to write with the right hand. Awkward as it was for the left-hander, his right-handed cursive turned out surprisingly legible.

There was corporal punishment in those days, and visiting pupils hear about it. They may hear the tale of the two cunning ne'er-do-wells sent off for a piece of hickory with which they'd receive their comeuppance. They returned with a twig. Sent out for something more substantial, they brought in a fence post. Sentence suspended; teacher spared the rod.

About halfway down the hill from the schoolhouse, Art and Ermadene Dickey presided over Greteman's General Store. It was moved to Living History Farms in 1979, after serving the community of Willey, Iowa, for nearly a century.

A bright red coffee grinder stands among barrels of coffee and crackers in the center of the store. To the right of the door an ornate grille rises above the post office counter. Glass-enclosed cases display pocketknives and spectacles. Shelves hold canned goods, perfumed soap, bolts of cloth, and button shoes. Beyond the timeworn chairs near the potbellied stove, pitchforks and scythes hang on the back wall. The revolution in technology and transportation had just begun the flood of factory wares.

"The general store served as more than just the shopping mall of the 1870s," Art told me, tipping back his black bowler hat and adjusting his sleeve garter. "It was the meeting place for town and country. Here was the center for news and gossip. The storekeeper's extension of credit and acceptance of produce in barter was also important, because there just wasn't much cash around in those days."

"Don't forget the post office," added Ermadene. "When I step behind that counter, I represent the full authority of the federal government." Also, by the late 1870s, mail order houses offered a wide variety of goods that had to be delivered here. Even the most isolated farmer could use a "wish book."

By the turn of the 20th century the farms of the Middle West were established and, for the most part, prosperous. Fields of tall corn cracked and rustled where once prairie wild flowers bloomed. At the 1900 Farm section of Living History Farms, white pickets fence the dooryard of a white frame farmhouse; to the right stand the neat red barn and corncrib. Beyond the post-mounted dinner bell a windmill clatters, pumping water.

The two-story house reflects the prosperity of this farm—a far cry from the log cabin and split-rail fences of fifty years earlier. Horses and laborsaving machinery—from steel plows and riding planters to double-row cultivators—enable these farmers to grow more than enough food for the farm family—enough to sell for cash, enough to feed the nation's increasing number of city dwellers.

A potbellied stove, gleaming with polish, warms the parlor. Rag rugs cover the floor; a pump organ stands in the corner, and occasionally a visitor pulls the stool up to the keyboard and sends the organ's rich music ringing through the house. On a table next to the window lies a stereoscope. Drop a card into this wondrous device and gaze upon three-dimensional images of the River Nile and the Great Pyramid of Cheops.

From the dining room comes the fragrance of bread baking in the wood-fueled stove. No longer does the farm wife have to rely on her Dutch oven for baking. I walk through the pantry; shining Mason jars of string beans, tomatoes, and pickles, grown on this farm and canned here, burden the shelves. In the

kitchen Donna Wishman washes bowls in a dishpan at the dry sink.

Out in the field the harvest is still under way. I walk between rustling rows of corn toward three men. A steady *thunk thunk* accompanies their progress down the row as they pull off ears, husk them, and toss them into a wagon drawn by a team of draft horses. The horses move forward to keep up with the trio, without command, stepping a few feet in a jingle of harness.

"We've had a really good crop this year," farm manager Ron Westphal tells me as he works. "We plant the old varieties of corn—not the hybrids—and we got 70 bushels an acre." A man with a strong, gentle face, Ron takes off the husking hook and invites me to try it. I buckle it on, a fingerless glove for the right hand. At the base of the thumb, a steel spur riveted to the leather points at an angle toward my fingertips.

Ron shows me how to grasp an ear of corn with my left hand, twist it off the stalk, and then catch the steel spur under the husk and tear it off. Ron and his practiced helpers work with an easy, natural motion, hardly pausing as they walk down the row. I have to stop and concentrate. It is hard work.

We reach the end of the row, and it's time to head for the corncrib; the wagon is full. I glance across the field.

Golden stalks stretch into the distance where once tall prairie grasses waved. By 1900 the rich soil of the grasslands had become America's breadbasket.

My quest is ended. I have traveled across the land and across the centuries to discover the rural legacy of an earlier America, its skills and achievements as awesome as those of our own mechanized world.

Vineyard terraces, first cultivated a century ago, slope past Chateau Chevalier in California's Napa Valley. The vines yield mostly Cabernet Sauvignon, the grape of California's proudest reds and of the storied French chateaus of Bordeaux. Chateau Chevalier itself resembles a French castle, but one near Amboise in the Loire country.

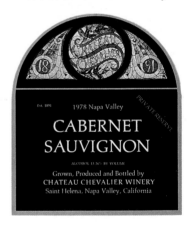

The label mirrors the stained glass in the main entrance, where owner Greg Bissonette tests the sugar content of grape juice before fermentation.

FOLLOWING PAGES: Woodcarver's gallery in the California cellars of Sebastiani Vineyards displays a centuries-old art. With mallet and chisels Earle Brown engraves a 50-gallon wine barrel, one of hundreds he has embellished.

CHUCK O'REAR (ABOVE AND OPPOSITE). WINE LABEL FROM CHATEAU CHEVALIER

An Ozark Craft: "It's Almost Gone, Really"

The way Irene Haymes heard it, Indians taught the early settlers how to weave corn-shuck seats for furniture. Down through the generations the craft has all but disappeared from the Ozark country; in fact, Irene Haymes

Bittersweet

thinks she's the only one left who has the know-how. And here she passes it on, winding corn shucks into a thin rope— while husband, Wilford, whose grandfather settled this farm in 1839, canes a stool seat.

Observing the handiwork, high school reporters of Lebanon, Missouri, take it all down for the pages of Bittersweet, a periodical that seeks to document a fading way of life in the Ozarks.

Cities That Show Their

Splendid mansions restore 19th-century elegance to the historic district in Charleston, South Carolina,

Age – Proudly

By Gene S. Stuart
Photographs by Ethan Hoffman

the city that pioneered 20th-century urban preservation.

Nature turns brutal, and rural and small-town folk, who live more intimately with its whims than do city dwellers, mark the event as a memorable date. Beside the Ohio River, in Madison, Indiana, more than one person observed that my visit coincided with just such a significant occasion. They delighted in the telling.

"This is the anniversary of the great tornado. It was April 3, 1974. Blew the roof off the library of Hanover College. Uprooted trees. Lot of damage, but it didn't come down here. Eight years ago today." Then they would pause and add the news that "they've issued another tornado warning this morning."

All day we watched the turbulent blackening sky above the town and the high hill behind it. Trees flailed the wind and gossamer veils of rain billowed through the streets. We could feel unbalance and violence in the air. Luckily, the twisting deadly storms missed Madison once more. But I shall always remember the third of April 1982 for another reason. It was the day the muddy river flowed the wrong way.

"Does this happen often?" I asked. "Are those whitecaps normal?"

"Browncaps," a wiry, matter-of-fact man corrected with a twinkle. "No. I've been watching the river 40 years and I never saw the wind blow it upstream."

Madisonians have always watched the river. Indeed, they owe the existence of the town to it. In the late 18th and early 19th centuries, pioneers came downstream by raft, flatboat,

or canoe, headed deeper into the old Northwest Territory. Many disembarked at a centuries-old river crossing to take the Michigan Trail, an Indian route so long traveled it had been worn into the land. It was there on a narrow floodplain, nestled between the hills of Indiana Territory and Kentucky, that Madison began as a small settlement of log cabins.

I visited many towns and cities throughout the nation that had evolved from such simple beginnings: places that preserve one small building, a neighborhood, an entire town; places that preserve customs transplanted from older worlds or made into something significantly American. Everywhere, I saw how people nurtured the local past, and treasured it like a collective souvenir.

Madisonians, especially, savored the story of their town—of how the era of steam turned the Ohio into a two-way thoroughfare and Madison into an important stop on the route between Pittsburgh and New Orleans. Industries developed: shipyards, flour mills, ironworks, and a button factory among them. By 1850 the settlement had grown to a wealthy town of 8,000.

In local belief Madison served as "Hog Butcher for the World" long before Chicago inspired that claim by Carl Sandburg. The city thrived on its busy pork packinghouses. In 1851 Jenny Lind, the Swedish Nightingale, was booked to sing in a Madison packinghouse, to her dismay. The town lacked a proper hall for a large audience. No problem. According to a newspaper account, locals reasoned the packinghouse would hold 2,500

Renewing Charleston's past, David Cantey strips the John Morrison house to bare wood for repainting. The bald cypress, cut from nearby swamps, proved durable and decay resistant; the sea captain's house, mingling Georgian and Federal styles, has stood for nearly 180 years.

people since it had held that number of hogs at butchering time. Surely a human would take no more space than a dressed hog.

Despite such timely improvisation, those were days of elegance. Noted architects designed for Madison. Buildings reflected a variety of such stylistic tastes as Federal, Greek and Roman Revival, Gothic Revival, and Italianate. Greek Revival also reflected the attitude that Americans continued the democratic ideals of ancient Greece; banks, churches, and houses took on the dignity of classical temples. Artisans decorated many buildings with locally made ironwork and shipped more downriver. In high-ceilinged, crystal-chandeliered dining rooms citizens entertained with local delicacies.

"There were sturgeon in the river over five feet long," John Windle, a leader in Madison's preservation efforts, told me. "Madison dined on caviar grown in its own front yard."

Madison envisioned still another wealthy future in railroads. Location proved no deterrent. Entrepreneurs cut a route through the limestone hills and built one of the first railways west of the Alleghenies. At first teams of horses pulled cars (containing men, women, or dressed hogs) up an awesome grade to the plateau above, gaining 413 feet in just over a mile. A few years later a center rail with ratchets and an engine fitted with a cogwheel walked trains uphill. Finally, a powerful steam engine performed the task.

But other railroad lines bypassed Madison. The town never became a rail center. According to a local saying, "Madison was the town that caught the boat but missed the train." And railroads meant the demise of steamboats. By 1860 the town's wealth had faded.

Madison dwindled in population and, in a sense, stopped in time. As years passed, its charm increased, for few places could boast such a variety of 19th-century architecture; 130 city blocks had been left virtually unaltered. The town's poverty helped preserve it. Few could afford to modernize or tear down and rebuild. In World War II a government-produced film featured Madison as the typical American town. Our fighting forces and allies visualized the heartbeat of America here—a little town in the heart of the country. After seeing it, a Michigan museum curator pleaded, "Put a fence around the entire town and don't let anyone touch anything in it!"

"Madison lay dormant a hundred years," says courtly, white-haired John Windle. And Madison credits John with its awakening. In 1960 John and a group of concerned people founded Historic Madison, Inc., which now owns eight buildings. In 1973 the entire town below the hill was listed in the National Register of Historic Places.

The National Trust for Historic Preservation selected Madison as a pilot town in its Main Street Project, an attempt to revive ghostly downtown areas haunted by thriving outlying shopping centers. In Madison's case, the modern developments have grown up on top of the hill. The Main Street program aims for economic development within the context of historic preservation.

Merchants of Madison have sought to make their storefront signs more compatible with the old facades, and the overall effort seems to take the business district back a century.

Frank Hurdis, Jr., director of Historic Madison, and I walked through the town in that tender time of spring when trees leaf pale green; on the dappled sidewalks there is a chill in shade and warm comfort in sunlight.

We visited Dr. William Hutchings' office, a simple, straightforward brick building with shuttered windows; office and waiting room below, two hospital rooms above, the beds made with the original sheets and blankets. When the doctor died in 1903, his daughters closed the building. It stayed that way for 70 years. His instruments, medicine bottles, and reference library lie in ordered array—as if the doctor had hurriedly saddled his horse and ridden away on call. Historic Madison maintains the office as a museum.

At the Schroeder Saddle Tree Factory, Frank and I pushed our way through long threads of cobwebs woven across dusty workbenches, carving tools, machines, a forge. Blades of sunlight pried through clapboard walls to probe the dim interior. More than a hundred wooden saddle frames sit neatly stacked, as if another shipment is ready for Europe, South America, or the U. S. Cavalry in World War I. Surely decades have not passed. . . . Surely the Schroeders will begin another working day tomorrow. . . .

The factory, too, will become a museum, for historians marvel at "one of the most complete preservations" of a 19th-century, one-family industry yet found in the nation.

Americans view such small towns with affection. They are our collective and idyllic grass roots. The social critic Thorstein Veblen thought country towns played "a greater part than any other in . . . giving character to American culture."

When idealized, all New England becomes a small town, living history dominated by tall church spires. A town of God, laws, and literature with a meeting hall and sturdy old houses bordering the peaceful village green. The South brings to mind magnolias abloom in a town square and an antebellum courthouse protected by a stone Confederate soldier on a pedestal. The Old West recalls tumbleweeds blowing through dusty streets past saloons, a hotel, and the livery stable in a ghost town, rich for perhaps only a decade and then abandoned. Many such towns do exist and have been at least partially preserved.

Cities have suffered more. As America's cities grew, they reflected an aura of wealth and culture, but industrialization in the 19th and 20th centuries tainted the image with scenes of squalor and crowding. Until recently the remedy for such ills has been to tear down the old and build anew in its place, a process of recycling that obliterated the past.

Now, in cities across the land, residents seek to revitalize the timeworn and neglected, pursuing 20th-century urbanity amid the look and style of an earlier day. The movement gained momentum during the 1950s and '60s, when preservationists increased efforts to prevent historic areas from being swept away by the bulldozer technique of renewal. By then, a model had already been established in Charleston, South Carolina.

The city sits on a low-lying peninsula at the confluence of the Ashley and Cooper Rivers and, like many old port cities, reflects cosmopolitan tastes and a singular atmosphere. Street vendors, portrayed in the opera *Porgy and Bess,* once called their wares as if in song, "I'm ta-a-alking about food I sell . . . SHE CRAB." They still do: "Da-a-affoDIL," they call. "Ri-i-ice basket." And graciously, women demonstrate how to fashion winnowing baskets from sea grass. Ships heavy-laden with goods once *(Continued on page 85)*

Savannah: Patterns of Elegance

Yearlong restoration banished decades of blight from the house built for Confederate Gen. Hugh Mercer. Pipe organ in the game room (left) and dark walls in a parlor add modern touches to a mansion that lives with history. Rough days of Sherman's march saw the house gutted as it stood, unfinished, on Monterey Square.

FOLLOWING PAGES: With paint and polish the concept of adaptive use transforms the ballroom of an 1893 armory into a library-gallery for the Savannah College of Art and Design.

Look What's Happened to Main Street:

Madison, Indiana, shows its colors boldly, accenting a heavy roof cornice and crowns on windows. High style a century ago, such facades fell from favor as uptown shops lured downtown shoppers, and Main Street—here and in countless towns across America—declined. Now old facades, back in style, help revive town centers. Paving brick in front of a Madison firehouse inspired the logo of the Main Street Project, which

hopes to prove that small-town preservation pays. An old-time Madisonian had little doubt; to him, downtown "never looked so fresh . . . so prosperous."

FOLLOWING PAGES: *Townsfolk meet for a talk and a trim at a Main Street barbershop. Flanking metal poles, notes owner Herschel Wheeler, have been painted like this ever since he and his dad opened 45 years ago. The cast-iron columns date to the mid-19th century.*

Heritage of Pleasure:
Playing New Orleans Jazz

called at the busy port. They still do that, too. The South Battery mansions near water's edge, with long windows and wide verandas, lure the slightest ocean breeze; and the pastel hues of Rainbow Row houses seem to catch and hold the brilliant glow of a low sun.

In 1838 English writer Fanny Kemble saw Charleston and was impressed by its eclectic architectural styles: "Every house seems built to the owner's particular taste; and in one street you seem to be in an old English town, and in another in some continental city of France or Italy. This variety is extremely pleasing to the eye."

But Charleston's grandeur faded. After the siege and defeat of the Civil War the gracious old port became a disheveled, unpainted, down-at-heels town. Some of its fine homes became noisy slum houses. One hovel was known as "Racket Hotel."

When novelist Henry James visited in 1905, he saw "an economic blight unrepaired" and Charleston's women as "rare, discreet, flitting figures that brushed the garden walls with noiseless skirts in the little melancholy streets of interspaced, overtangled abodes." DuBose Heyward, a native son, called it "an ancient beautiful city that time had forgotten before it destroyed." One short description aptly sums up: "a city of drifted yesterdays."

Susan Pringle Frost, another native, noted how collectors from "Everywhere Else" stripped mansions of iron railings and hand-carved paneling and ornament and shipped them away. "I can't stand it," she declared.

She began her campaign of preservation in 1909 by buying one house. She cleaned and painted it and bought another. "I repaired the old places as much as I could," she said. "Then I sought buyers or renters who could be trusted with what I knew were national treasures. This took doing! I remember how I put a first mortgage on one house; then a second; then a third loan. But the Fates were with me." She browsed through junkyards for iron gates and balconies from razed houses. Plumbers and contractors sympathetic to her cause alerted her to buildings about to be destroyed, and she salvaged ironwork, mantelpieces, woodwork, and ornaments. Many saw her as an impractical visionary; yet she personally saved more than 30 houses and devoted her life to historic Charleston.

The city enacted its pioneering historic district ordinance in 1931. Other organizations have taken up the cause, and Charleston is recapturing in spirit what Bostonian Josiah Quincy saw in 1773: "In grandeur, splendour of buildings, decorations, equipages . . . it far surpasses all I ever saw, or ever expected to see, in America."

Surpassing splendor. A visitor pauses at a tall iron gate allowing a long gaze to wander along a brick walkway through bright banks of azaleas. A visitor enters a mansion preserved. Gleaming furniture and shining silver, Charleston made, sit under watchful eyes of serene faces, Charleston portraits.

Charleston preservationists now protect more than 2,000 dwellings. Houses about to be razed are sometimes moved, refurbished, and sold. One group offered a dismantled

Jazz trumpeter Kid Thomas Valentine, who heard the driving brass of Louis Armstrong and King Oliver, listens to young Wendell Brunious in a front-porch session. The lively octogenarian still performs, endowing youth with the old music of sadness and celebration.

house free to anyone who would reassemble it within the Old and Historic District. Frances R. Edmunds, director of Historic Charleston Foundation, believes the city is nearing its long-sought goal of protection for the entire peninsula that cradled it.

How to approach the salvation of a building has often created controversy—whether to preserve it as it stands, to restore authentically, or to modernize. Purists may want as little as possible altered. Historian Charles B. Hosmer, Jr., reports a counter view: "If a person buys an old house, pays a lot of money for it, and intends to use it as a year-round home, he is not going to be satisfied to take his bath in a tin foot-tub and go to bed with a candle in one hand and a warming-pan in the other just for archaeological reasons."

Both Charleston and Savannah, Georgia, are southern seaports, but their origins differ. English aristocracy fostered the Charleston settlement, while the founding of Savannah was sparked by an idealist's dream of providing a new start for poor working people as well as an opportunity for mercantile groups.

In February of 1733 the social reformer and soldier James Edward Oglethorpe arrived in the new colony with 114 English settlers. They included 40 families—farmers and artisans, some who had paid their passage and others "who were render'd incapable of living at home . . . a parcel of poor people." They journeyed into the unknown fortified with swords, muskets, and ten casks "of Alderman Parson's best Beer."

Oglethorpe's was to be a colony free from slavery; it would prosper by growing silkworms. On a sandy bluff above the Savannah River he laid out his grand design, a town

of squares edged by public buildings and homes. Some say it was a scheme for military defense; in time it expanded into a superb series of squares celebrated by city planners.

By June the colony boasted nine frame houses and a smith's forge. Early in the century propagandists had promised "the most delightful country of the universe." But one resident wrote of "an abundance of torments, as Cock-roaches, Wood-ticks, Sand-flies, Moskettos, and other Vermin." Dreams faded. The silkworms failed. Despite Oglethorpe's plan, slavery arrived. But Europe's oppressed did come: English, Scots, Irish, Jews, Moravians, Salzburgers, Swiss, and Italians.

At times Savannah prospered through trade. From a poor 18th-century "wooden town built on a sand heap" it became a wealthy 19th-century port. King Cotton made Savannah a queen city of mansions and row houses, and Oglethorpe's grand design became a pattern of elegance.

At dawn, fog and fine mist hang in the air, damp reminders of the wide river and the sea. Blocks toward the waterfront change from flower-strewn parks to time-honored buildings and back again. A sense of countryside and city weave together to form Savannah beneath a canopy of trees until the last park ends. Soon, slippery cobbled ramps lead steeply to the river. It smells of fish and oil and swampland.

The sandy face of the bluff has gone, shored long ago with gray ballast stone offloaded at the port. Mist fades. Old offices and warehouses of Factors Walk, range upon range several stories tall, loom above. I have passed block after block of pleasant old houses and businesses, but these structures are serious, even austere. Cotton fortunes were made here. But now a woman hangs from a top-floor window, leaning from her modern apartment to greet a passing friend and welcome the strolling stranger with a friendly call and a wave. Fashionable boutiques and restaurants on the lower level begin to open. Savannah has saved and restored its ruined waterfront.

It was always boom or bust in the city. Early in the 20th century the boll weevil dethroned King Cotton, and Savannah slipped into poverty once more.

"We were too poor to tear down and modernize," preservationist Lee Adler II told me with a smile. "In the 1950s we looked at the city and realized the value of what we have. We organized, developed financial techniques. But success came from the dedication of the people. We attracted about a thousand families downtown. So many became financially involved that the preservation program became a success. We have 2½ square miles of historic buildings."

Just to the south lies the Victorian district, a 45-block, 19th-century suburb turned slum. Adler organized the Savannah Landmark Rehabilitation Project in 1974 to restore its gingerbread-millworked and balustraded frame houses without displacing the many low-income, mostly black residents.

In a downtown forge blacksmith-sculptor Ivan Bailey, young, strong, and dirt-smeared, hammered at a white-hot fleur-de-lis. His assistants assembled a metal fountain ornament, a tall water bird surrounded by graceful blades of grass. "The same techniques are used today in blacksmithing that were used in the old days," said Ivan. "But I wouldn't want to be a smith back then . . . without modern tools. Drudge work. But it was vital. In the

early days, a town could be a town without a church, but it couldn't be a town without a blacksmith." Old Savannah, certainly, would look far different without its iron gates and railings and balustrades.

We climbed into his pickup truck to jounce through the Victorian district, past ghost-gray weathered houses near collapse and sprightly restored dwellings. Ivan spoke of the Savannah of a century and more ago. "Many people had a carriage house and at least two horses," he said. "With dogs, cats, pigs, and chickens, imagine the summer stench. Savannah built houses with high stoops to be above the mosquitoes and road dirt."

We parked in a cloud of dust in front of the house he and his wife have redone with "shoestring restoration." Iron railings of his own design span the front. "I traded off labor with a neighbor who was restoring his house and did woodwork," Ivan told me.

"It's very gratifying," he added. "Young couples who restore their own homes use their recreation time to do something that's creatively satisfying. It gives a house meaning." We climbed out and surveyed his restoration, a jewel of a Victorian cottage. His proud grin changed to a laugh. "Thank God it's finished. You feel guilty if you don't work on it weekends. And you get so sick of it you don't want to touch it."

Like Savannah and Charleston, New Orleans owes its beginning to a propitious river site. It is daily dominated by its nurturing stream. The living hold the Mississippi back with earthen levees; the dead are held above its seeping ooze in tall tombs. It is a place over-vulnerable.

It is also a place of immediate pleasures. And people of Spain, *(Continued on page 94)*

House made of desert takes shape in Santa Fe, New Mexico. Workers mix mud mortar, lay adobe brick, and round a lofty stair support. Spanish settlers blended adobe techniques of the Old and New Worlds into styles continued by Santa Fe preservationists.

FOLLOWING PAGES: *Candles aglow in paper bags—called* farolitos, *little lanterns—shed the light and warmth of Christmas in Santa Fe. Two* luminarias, *or bonfires, symbolize the shepherds' watch in the fields near Bethlehem.*

France, Africa, and the West Indies blended traditions to give it a culture of its own and a love of festivity, food, dance, and music.

Ramble along Bourbon Street in the French Quarter. Melody pours from clubs and cabarets. Stop for a night or a song. Listen to the soul of the city—New Orleans music.

A small group spotlighted on a raised bandstand plays old hits, marches, hymns. Anything can be jazz. It's a way of playing a song. The crowd begins to move, sway, shout encouragement. The band moves a song this way and that within the jazz pattern. Version after version of the theme, ever changing. A trumpet wails the pain of it, a trombone growls. A piano and then a clarinet embroider around the tune. They drive. The crowd is inspired. On its feet. Calling. Clapping. The band takes the song home, fragmenting, flowing together again, music thrumming through the hall and into the street. And behind it all a bass struts stylized musical steps along the parade of melody.

It all came together here at the Crescent City on the Mississippi in the waning 19th century—strands of West African music, Caribbean themes, and European harmonies woven into a new music, American music. Inspiration came from many sources, but black musicians played a preeminent role.

There was variety in jazz to fit a mood, a special occasion—blues, stomps, rags, funerals. Buddy Bolden, its first legend, began his rise back in the late 1890s. They said you could hear his cornet across the river. It's believable. It's possible. If he made recordings, none survive. But those who had heard him said his blue notes "sounded like his heart was breaking." Musicians learned from him and from each other, playing "mighty much

by head." If they called you King, you were the best. If they called you Kid, you might be crown prince—and the name might stick until you were old and gray.

King Oliver, Jelly Roll Morton, and other greats played in Storyville, a notorious district of dance halls, saloons, and "sporting houses." During World War I, under pressure from the Secretary of the Navy, reluctant city fathers banned the bordellos. Legend has it that the crackdown dispersed the jazzmen. But many had never played in Storyville, and by 1917 a lot of players had already left New Orleans. They went to cities on the Mississippi, to Chicago and New York, west to California. Regional styles developed, and the music gave its name to the carefree Jazz Age.

Tastes in popular music changed, sending the traditional jazz temporarily into eclipse. But by the end of World War II the old music was back in favor. Some of the old-timers were rediscovered. Someone had found the aging Bunk Johnson and bought him a set of teeth. He began his comeback with a cornet he described as "just a little bit better than a coffee pot." George Lewis played with "a clarinet he held together with wire, rubber bands, and hardened chewing gum."

Allan Jaffe helped establish Preservation Hall in 1961 "so the old musicians would have a place to play and be heard and appreciated." Its home is in a 150-year-old building in the French Quarter. Jazz pianist and singer Alton Purnell was born there and occasionally performs in the hall. A long, tropical patio separates the hall from Jaffe's office, a room cluttered with jazz posters, instruments, and parts of band uniforms. It was late, and wisps of music and applause drifted back to us as Allan spoke of the performers.

Log vigas and corbels bear witness to a dual heritage in Santa Fe's modern-day county courthouse. Vigas, or roof beams, trace to prehistoric Pueblo dwellings; painted and carved corbels derive from Spanish colonial architecture.

"For these musicians in their 70s and 80s to still be playing, touring, they have to still be enjoying it," says Allan, who himself enjoys sitting in at the tuba. "They've all seen hard times. These are the survivors.

"Young musicians still learn through apprenticeship. We've kept the tradition long enough for them to hear it. They feel respect for the music and want to learn the old way, within the form. Here, they might get a chance to sit in. Kid Thomas Valentine is one of the most influential in teaching. He has patience with young players. He'll sit up all night at a jam session—and he's 86.

"New Orleans jazz was created to serve a need—the people's own music. It was music to dance by, have funerals by, and have parades by, all with the same musicians. If a band played for a funeral and didn't make somebody cry, they weren't hired again. If they played for a dance and didn't make people want to dance, they weren't hired again. Jazz only functions as long as it continues to serve a need of the people."

Inside the hall, the audience filled wooden benches and crowded against the walls. I settled just outside the room on a church pew in the corridor. The music began again.

An elderly white-haired man in a white suit entered from the street and paused. Raindrops lay upon his hair. In the dim light from a naked bulb high above, he seemed to glow with an aura, silhouetted against the night. His companion led him to sit beside me. He turned his face up as if to see. The music swirled around us. Within seconds the world-renowned Argentine writer, Jorge Luis Borges, in New Orleans to receive an academic honor, was lost in the listening, a look of delighted surprise in his sightless eyes.

The players chose notes as explicit as words. They chose well, played against one another and with each other. The sound convoluted, soaring from Preston Jackson's trombone, rambling from Emma Barrett's piano. As a solo run ended, players complimented expertise with a quick jerk of the head, an approving glance. Pleased with an entire song, they exchanged looks, slapped their knees, snapped their fingers, exclaimed, "Ye-a-a-h-h." They were playing hot, and they knew it. The crowd wanted to dance, wanted to cry. It drowned the band with waves of applause. Borges's smile held a look of understanding and approval. It was an inspired choice of place. People playing honest music of long tradition had shown him the essence of the city.

Spirit of place in one city may be an abomination in another. An irate editorialist once likened a glaring sign in front of a colonial church "in beautiful and artistic Santa Fe" to a "jazz band in the Choir Invisible."

While Spain left its influence on New Orleans, it made Santa Fe a Spanish-American city. Settlers, soldiers, and missionaries of Renaissance Spain founded it in 1610 as the capital of the "Kingdom of New Mexico." They named it the town of Holy Faith—Santa Fe; and they built it in a severe landscape near mountains that assume a sanguine hue in long sunlight. Sangre de Cristo they called them, Blood of Christ. Late in the 17th century the town chose St. Francis of Assisi as its patron.

Settlers drew from their traditions and those of the local Pueblo Indians to create a new kind of architecture. They surrounded

Spanish patios with flat-roofed Pueblo rooms made of sun-dried adobe brick and mud plaster. The art of brickmaking came from the Old World—the Moors had introduced it to arid Spain. The plaster was applied by hand, in the fashion of the Pueblo people.

This Spanish-Pueblo style echoes the color and form of the hills and mountains, whether red-lit in a fiery sunset or softened by a rumpled blanket of snow.

In the mid-1800s the style evolved to Santa Fe Territorial, with fired-clay bricks topping adobe walls, graceful millwork, and painted trim. But by 1868 a newspaper complained of outdated provincial adobe and its tendency to dissolve in rain: "The consequence is nearly every roof in the town has considered it a special privilege to leak like a sieve. . . . homes are made uncomfortable, housewives are without good humor, and all because our people persist in the antiquated custom of piling *dirt* upon their roofs instead of building good shingle or board roofs to their houses."

Santa Fe went modern with clay brick, stained glass, turrets, and jigsaw work. Yet, in the 1920s and '30s, people converted many of these Victorian buildings and covered them with stucco for a newly fashionable adobe look. Today Santa Fe protects and preserves the original adobe styles. Designer Bill Field inherited his grandmother's adobe house. "You can't imagine the work involved maintaining it," he told me. "Something must be done to adobe every year—patching, replacing. It never really stops."

"There is a tremendous renaissance right now in building with adobe," Pedro Ribera Ortega commented. "Interestingly enough, it returned through the hippies wanting to get back to the earth. You can't get any closer to earth than adobe." We sat near the end of the old Santa Fe Trail in the heart of the city. Pedro, an educator and scholar of New Mexico history, was born no more than a quarter of a mile from here. Both branches of his family had come to New Mexico in 1598; by 1620 they were in Santa Fe. "We Hispanic New Mexicans," he told me, "are people with profound roots. They are just a part of us. It is a very beautiful sense of belonging to a land. . . . You are part of the earth. We obviously looked to the Indians, absorbing that feeling. Our attitude is: The earth is part of our inheritance, you have to take care of it. But they start on a much deeper religious level."

Both Indians and Hispanics evidence a deep sense of tradition in craftsmanship and celebration. Spanish settlers brought large flocks of sheep, adding wool to the Indians' rich heritage of weaving. Pueblo Indians and early settlers built a system of *acequias*—irrigation ditches—that are still painstakingly maintained by their descendants. And in religious processions in small towns and Indian pueblos around Santa Fe celebrants carry *santos*—images of saints—hand-carved in the tradition of their ancestors.

Every autumn the Fiesta de Santa Fe celebrates Hispanic heroes and heritage as it has for 270 years. Pedro works months in the planning; year round he collects folklore and history. Some New Mexicans, he notes, still use phraseology and manners of old Spain and Mexico. He has heard villagers in the hills singing medieval ballads. "The oldest European mystery play for Christmas is about the Three Kings," says Pedro. "It dates back to the 12th century. In Spain they only study it as literature, but we put it on each year.

"Our Christmas celebration is a season of

pageantry that is unique, combining Spanish, Indian, Mexican, and Anglo traditions. It is a sharing of customs. Ours is a very beautiful cultural mix, all four respecting each other's traditions and yet united in one."

Spaniards named a California mission for St. Francis, but the town that grew there did not remain Spanish. The United States is a "nation of nations," and San Francisco reflects that. Among the peoples who came here were the Chinese; they too, as the Spaniards had, sought wealth in the New World.

They called California "Golden Mountain" for the promise it held and came dreaming of making their fortunes. Between 1910 and 1940 officials detained the immigrants on hilly Angel Island in San Francisco Bay. For most, San Francisco's Golden Gate eventually opened onto Golden Mountain. A few languished for months in the island barracks only to be deported.

Plans to raze the abandoned immigration building stopped in 1970 after a park ranger investigated graceful Chinese characters carved and written on the walls. They proved to be more than 135 poems written by detainees, silent cries of the desperate. Some speak of bitterness, some of heartbreak:

My parents are old; my family is poor.
Cold weather comes; hot weather goes.
Heartless white devils,
Sadness and anger fill my heart.

Today Angel Island is a state park, recent California history preserved, and Chinese Americans look to it as part of their heritage.

People of San Francisco's Chinatown hold to ancient traditions of immigrant ancestors.

As the Year of the Rooster (1981) ended and the Year of the Dog was about to begin, I presented red flowers to the patriarch of the Quock family, Mr. Quock Fat. The color wished him well in the coming year. His smile spread so with kindness it closed his delighted eyes. For an evening I joined him and his more Americanized family in an age-old celebration. Quock is a retired chef and had prepared a feast to close the old year.

"I'm Hank, number one son," the eldest greeted me. Quock has sons numbering three and daughters numbering six. Sons, daughters, husbands, wives, and their offspring gathered for the dinner.

"There are 31 of us here," said Frances Quock Chinn. "But this is a small family dinner; 25 more are missing."

At each place lay ivory chopsticks. As I tried to master the unfamiliar tools, my new friends praised the effort when sea urchins wobbled to my mouth, politely ignored me when specially prepared seaweed plopped into my lap. They explained the significance of course after course. "Each ingredient in every dish has a meaning," explained Hank, who is also a skilled cook. Shrimps, or *ha,* stand for "the sound of laughter." A chopped chicken is carefully rearticulated because "everything must have a beginning and an end." A crisp vegetable expresses a hope "that you will have many sons."

After the feast ended and as each family left, the oldest daughter, the mother of ten, presented them with a one-layered pudding to eat on Chinese New Year's Day. "In China it is different. It has nine layers. Nine means forever, or long life," explained daughter-in-law Hilda Quock. Hank told me the celebration goes on for days with *(Continued on page 105)*

City Within a City
Honors Oriental Origins

Tangerines tempt shoppers in San Francisco's Chinatown during lunar New Year celebrations. Gat, the fruit's Chinese name, signifies good fortune. Festivals and family feasts embrace revered traditions of the Orient. California's gold fields lured the first immigrants; they knew bitter rejection, yet built railroads, turned swampland into farmland, and eventually added their odyssey and their culture to the American mosaic. In language and architecture East and West meet on busy Grant Avenue (opposite), heart of one of the largest Chinese communities outside Asia.

FOLLOWING PAGES: *Silk-clad scholar Kenneth Joe nurtures his centuries-old heritage in an Oriental setting. In Chinese calligraphy, he brushes a poem of homesickness and of time and changing seasons.*

Comeback of a Company Town

Ablaze again with festive light, the Hotel Florence in Pullman, Illinois, rises near the site where George Pullman produced his famed railroad cars. He built the hotel, named it for a favorite daughter, and surrounded it with what he envisioned as a model company town, the hotel a haven for the elite. His rules and labor's unrest shattered the plans. Today's residents revive the town, now blended into Chicago. Hotel doors boast original Victorian fittings.

The Enduring Charm of Old Cape May

the onset of the new year. "My father came from China and likes the old traditions," Hank added. "We respect his wishes."

Of the thousands of Chinese immigrants who sailed into San Francisco Bay, many must have gazed perplexed at a glowing sign that dominated the waterfront. Ghirardelli, it proclaimed. If anyone explained its significance to the immigrants, they must have been amazed, assured indeed that this was a land of plenty, for their introduction to the wondrous land of golden mountains was the massive sign for a chocolate factory.

The brick complex seemed destined for destruction until investors in the 1960s converted it into a mall of specialty shops, gardens, and restaurants. This approach proved that adaptive use of commercial buildings was practical. Boston proved reuse profitable in the East by saving Faneuil Hall, the historic market and civic center built in 1742, and several nearby buildings. They, too, house food shops, restaurants, specialty shops, and offices. Today hardly a city is without such a reclaimed commercial building of now fashionable exposed bricks, wide-planked floors, and hanging ferns.

Saving one building can be a formidable undertaking, but in the south side of Chicago the people of Pullman, Illinois, are trying to save an entire town. George M. Pullman built it in the 1880s as a model factory town, which would be good for his workers and good for his railroad car business.

Those were times of labor disturbances and social unrest. Factory workers often lived with poverty and disease in filthy tenements. Pullman envisioned an ideal town of healthy, productive employees, and he built a complete community around his new factory. It was America's "first all-brick city"; with a parklike setting and man-made lake, it was hailed as the "world's most perfect town."

The Hotel Florence, in Queen Anne style, housed visiting dignitaries. Workers shopped at the Arcade, joined the library, attended the theater. But the millennium had not yet arrived. The library charged a fee; no worker could buy a house. To some the atmosphere smacked of feudalism. When working hours and take-home pay dropped and fees and rents did not, 3,000 angered workers walked out in 1894. One newspaper commented: "Pullman is called a 'model town.' It now has on its hands a model strike."

A dream had sparked a nightmare, which history records as one of the bloodiest disputes in the labor union movement. By 1907 most of the property had indeed been sold to individuals, but the vision of the perfect town continued to fade.

Eventually Chicago neighborhoods encircled it. In the 1960s Pullman residents defeated a plan to demolish the entire town. It became a National Historic Landmark district in the 1970s, and its restoration continues.

Young, dark-haired Deborah Bertoletti said, "We've lived in Pullman eight years and we're restoring our second house. A lot of younger people are moving in. Here you know everybody. We work on our houses. It keeps us all together."

Storied Victorian verandas face seaward in Cape May, New Jersey. As the "Queen of the Seaside Resorts," it lured the wealthy with cool breezes and wide beaches. These beachfront houses withstood storms, fires, neglect; the town now protects them as treasured relics.

As we strolled Deborah's baby along tree-lined streets, an old man rebuilding his modernized porch back to 1880s style stopped hammering to smile and chat. A young couple painted trim on a row house facade. Many residents restore houses in red and green, traditional Pullman colors. Deborah lives in one of the three-story executive houses near the wide lawns of the Hotel Florence.

Here hotel manager Glenn Anderson presides with affection for the wide-verandaed, gabled treasure and for the town that spreads beyond it. "Many of us have lived here all our lives," he said. "My great-grandfather came here from Sweden as a brickmason. He helped build Pullman. When it was finished, he stayed. It's home."

The hotel's dining room has opened once more to reclaim an era. Waitresses in long skirts and high-necked, leg-o'-mutton-sleeved blouses glide among tables covered with white napery. The guest rooms will open again. Glenn and I walked up the wide, balustraded stairs to view ornate Victorian furnishings and stencil designs painted on walls —and to peer into the elegant suite George Pullman reserved for prideful visits to what he hoped would be a utopian venture.

The Pullmans, who owned several family homes, usually summered at their estate on the New Jersey shore. I, too, headed to the Jersey shore as the season turned, to see a once fashionable resort now restored to its original Victorian charm. There at Cape May, American Presidents escaped from political duties, the wealthy elite gathered for "the season," and those climbing to money and power came to watch and be watched.

Horses drew bathhouses to the water's edge, and ladies in pantaloons, short dresses, and bathing shoes emerged to trip into the waves. Those more modest had bathhouses drawn into the water and splashed in sequestered privacy. John Philip Sousa's band gave concerts. In 1906 Henry Ford and Louis Chevrolet raced motorcars on the strand.

Cape May boasted hotels of massive scale. The Mount Vernon was said to be the largest in the world; the dining room stretched longer than a football field.

Hotel and house architecture varied, with styles including Gothic Revival, Queen Anne, Italianate, Romanesque, and Second Empire. Many were sensible Shingle style, usually darkly hooded with a gabled roof. Some were decorated with a wooden overlay—the Stick style. Builders often combined several styles at whim. Local carpenters used pattern books as guides to construct some of the houses. With the invention of the jigsaw came intricate gingerbread woodwork, ornament for the showy summer homes of the new-rich. The resort took on a look of row upon row of giant wooden wedding cakes. On tranquil summer afternoons, ladies in lacy hats and collars reposed on verandas framed in lacy arches and balustrades.

The resort endured devastating fires in the 1800s, and in the 1900s it slipped into decline. The sea rhythmically reclaimed the beach with erosive tides. Then, in the changing perceptions of the 1960s, Cape May came to appreciate what a treasure it had in the handsome old buildings. "Our future is in our past," became the town motto. Residents made Cape May a Victorian resort in a modern world.

Bruce Minnix, a tall, sandy-haired man with the penetrating eyes of an observer, served as mayor while it was happening in the 1970s.

"Not everyone wanted the town restored," he recalled. "There were battles. But preservation meant increased tourism and economic recovery." He paused and smiled. "A town, after all, has to pay for itself."

Today a more informal vacationer returns yearly to socialize on Victorian porches. But there are still touches of elegance past. In one hotel, attendants whisk children to a separate dining room while parents, dressed in the latest resort fashions, dine quietly beneath slowly turning fans.

Well into the 20th century—not many decades away from Victorian tastes, but a world apart in appearances—a new design movement swept in. Art Deco took its name from a 1925 Paris exposition entitled "Exposition Internationale des Arts Décoratifs et Industriels Modernes."

The new movement would shun the past, strip away curlicues, and replace them with a lean, clean, streamlined salute to the machine age future. In time ocean liners took on a sleeker look. Swept-back train engines and automobiles appeared to be going fast when they were standing still. Angles turned to curves in everything from tableware to jewelry to interior design and architecture. Chrome, colored mirrors, and opaque glass decorated gas stations and skyscrapers alike.

In the mid-1930s Miami Beach broke out with its own version of Art Deco: stuccoed, pastel-painted hotels—confections in concrete. The resort looked like an outsize table with gigantic pastries to celebrate a Buck Rogers birthday.

Miami Beach was a place to escape the depression of the 1930s, a place where one hoped to see handsome men and platinum-haired beauties in white satin gowns slink across the dance floor to romantic rhythms. Dreams manifested themselves in etched mirrors and windows. On them, large full moons perpetually silhouetted swaying palms, and flamingos paused forever in mid-stride.

People from northern cities wintered in Miami Beach as "snowbirds," and some have fulfilled a dream of retiring there. Many live in the square-mile Art Deco District, one of the youngest in the National Register of Historic Places. Preservationists work to restore the district and save it from new developments, for it is a distinct neighborhood within the city and contains one of the largest arrays of Art Deco architecture in the nation.

Young people, artists, writers, and those seeking a view of aging fantasy now join octogenarians as Art Deco residents and discover an older generation's look to the future. And the young have taken a leading role in the spirited and sometimes bitter battle to save the Art Deco District.

It seems so recent, but it was during World War II that my family first drove to Miami Beach. To a little girl from a small town it was a land of Oz, and the Art Deco Victor Hotel, the wizard's palace. It is not so much that I have grown since then. The Victor has somehow shrunk. But the magic is still there. I would like to show it to my children.

If each generation rediscovers and reinterprets the American story, then we are curators of both past and present. I was reminded of the tenuous existence of our creations by an archaeologist friend. I had assumed him to be attuned only to the ancient, but one day he told me, "Always remember, the past begins with yesterday."

Cape May breakfast means a gracious table in the Victorian dining room of the Mainstay Inn. Says owner Sue Carroll, setting out the flowers: "The sideboard, mirrors, dining table, and brass chandelier are original pieces. The window treatments were made by me." Built in 1872 as a gambling club for gentlemen, the house regains its air of dated dignity with Sue and Tom Carroll's restoration. Wooden lace and rockers (opposite) invite reading and relaxing on the hexagonal porch at Poor Richard's Inn, a house in the Second Empire style with emphasis on symmetry. Local builders often designed houses themselves, applying jigsawed trim—which they could choose from pattern books—to balustrades and eaves. They combined styles into Victorian hybrids for the height of Cape May fashion—admired today as grass roots architecture.

BOTH BY STEPHANIE MAZE

Poor Richard's
Inn

Teamwork and tradition steer the Coast Guard bark Eagle *on a training cruise off New York. In heavy*

Ships of Wood

By Leslie Allen
Photographs by Ira Block

going cadets man three wheels to hold the 295-foot three-master on course.

The President of the Pacific Ocean abruptly fell silent. He stood up, slammed the front door, returned to his seat, and started talking again. "That's the ghost who lives here," he said with a deadpan look. "He was the first skipper I went to sea with, in a sailing ship, back in 1924. He opens doors—locked doors—and windows."

And the President? He was Philip "Spike" Africa, age 76, seaman under sail, maritime tradesman, artist, raconteur, and honorary statesman. He explained his title: "In every port, I'd get letters from my brother addressed to the President of the Pacific Ocean, and it hung on. It's not elective, just handed down. Now I only take care of tides and currents and mermaids. I protect the whales—little odd jobs, you know."

There are many ghosts of the sea in the life of Spike Africa. Few people today remember America's final days of commercial sail in the 1920s and '30s. Spike lived for them. From his boyhood home in Ohio he beat his way across the country, determined to seek his fortune on the lumber ships that sailed out of Portland, Oregon. "The shipping master called me a runt, but he finally shipped me on this five-masted schooner. I spent four years on her. But it was the end of an age, and I never got another ship after her."

Steady rain drummed the roof of Spike's home in Kirkland, near Seattle, Washington; he tucked a pinch of snuff inside his cheek and continued: "Two and a half million feet of timber on board, from Portland to Peru, on that first trip. One hundred and eight days down; one calm lasted three weeks. We had oil lamps, a wood cookstove, no machinery at all. But it was a great clean life—paucity of food and plenty of work." He spoke of the terror of going aloft in gales, of the forest of masts that was Seattle's waterfront.

Later, Spike worked as stevedore, fisherman, logger. The exquisitely precise macrame he learned as a seaman—"not those plant hangers you see today"—now brings income from the seafood restaurants he decorates. And throughout it all, he's wished that he'd been born in another, earlier time.

What, I wondered, has been lost?

"Peace," Spike replied. "Peace and quiet. Plus the determination of man to live with the elements. You can't conquer them, but you can live with them."

To listen to Spike Africa was to sense the fragility of our maritime heritage. The way of life he and countless others once pursued is gone forever. Wind and water, time and neglect conspire against old sailing ships, riverboats, waterfronts, lighthouses, and other artifacts of the past. Robbed of purpose, the time-honed subtleties of such skills as building wooden boats also become perishable. So do lore and tradition.

Yet America is the child of its maritime past. Ships brought explorers and later settlers, and linked the fledgling colonies to each other and the rest of the world. In the 19th century seafaring skill and commercial ingenuity took the United States and its products around the world; ships returned

To the count of a cadence-chanting seaman, cadets brace Eagle's *main yards on a port tack. With more than 20 miles of rigging and 20,000 square feet of sail,* Eagle *demands more expert seamanship, according to the Coast Guard, than its most technically advanced cutters.*

Labor and leisure alternate in Eagle's *round-the-clock routine. At the helm Cadet Third Class Meredith Austin intently eyes the compass as she steers. Cadets relaxing off watch practice a bit of marlinespike seamanship—shipboard knotting and splicing techniques. Gaining increasing expertise during several short cruises, cadets eventually learn to run the ship with little aid from the regular crew.*

laden with foreign goods, fresh ideas, and immigrants. By 1807 American vessels, most of them registered for foreign trade, already numbered about ten thousand. A decade later, steamboats were carrying Americans into their own heartland, where rivers and lakes became watery highways. Whalers and packets stand for a time of national optimism; the clipper ships, speeding along under acres of snowy canvas, remain powerful emblems of national pride.

None of the globe-girdling American clippers of the mid-19th century survive today. But in the past few decades, other old ships have been saved and restored, and reproductions of still others have been built. Their great hulls and soaring spars grace the waterfronts of dozens of cities. More important, they evoke a heritage. A ship properly set up as a museum or on display sends out emanations of lore, humanity, history, adventure, geography, art, and literature, says Karl Kortum, chief curator of San Francisco's National Maritime Museum and for many years a leading figure in maritime preservation.

Yet, museum ships are but one part of the effort. Preservation projects involve large and small craft, powered by sail, steam, diesel, and oar. Other efforts focus on lighthouses, waterfronts, skills, and traditions. So seriously does the United States Coast Guard take seamanship under sail that, in 1946, it commissioned a German-built square-rigger as its main training vessel for Coast Guard Academy cadets. During their four years at the Academy in New London, Connecticut, the officer trainees spend at least six weeks on the three-masted bark *Eagle*. "Sailing on *Eagle* provides basic learning that's applicable to even the most technically advanced ships," says her commanding officer, Capt. Martin J. Moynihan. "It also develops teamwork, camaraderie, leadership, and pride."

Reasons for maritime preservation range from the purely practical to the unashamedly nostalgic. There is usually a love of fine craftsmanship present—and often, an ear for the rhythms of nature. Everywhere I went, I sensed an effort to rediscover the *logic* of a maritime past—for use in the present.

That logic is perhaps nowhere as tangible as in the vicinity of Bath, Maine. On a map, the whole area resembles a gnarled hand, its fingers chiseled by rivers coursing into the Atlantic. Coves and rocky islands share the deep, broad reaches and estuaries that have defined maritime ways of life for nearly 400 years.

The first known wedding of sail and wood in the colonies took place here, in 1607. In that year, when Jamestown was founded far to the south, another band of English subjects arrived at the mouth of the Kennebec River and established the Popham Colony. Late in the year shipwrights set to work framing a 30-ton pinnace. When the settlement disbanded the following year, the colonists sailed the pinnace back to England.

But the seed of Kennebec River shipbuilding had been planted. By 1800 more than a hundred vessels had slid from Kennebec shipways; in mid-century, Maine led all the other states in shipbuilding, and Bath was reported to have more than a score of yards at work. Later in the century, Bath yards turned out the largest, and often the finest, wooden square-riggers ever built.

"A Bath man can no more help building

ships than he can help breathing," reported the *New York Marine Journal* in 1891. In countless nearby coves, an amazing variety of small craft was slowly evolving for fishing, lobstering, and local commerce.

The feel of its maritime past still pervades Bath. Snow piled high during my visit reminded me of the hardy self-sufficiency that built the city—a reminder reinforced by the portraits of stern-faced sea captains. The rounded steeples and bow windows of churches and homes reflected the shipbuilder's love of curving lines. The century-old Bath Iron Works was about to launch a naval frigate.

In a reconstructed sail loft on the Kennebec, I watched two young men discuss the correct placement of the tiller in a traditional wooden lobster boat called a peapod. The boat had a special beauty that comes from the graceful melding of form and function—and the skilled craftsman's union of hand and eye. Overlapping cedar planks traced clean lines over steam-bent oaken frames. Applewood, persuaded into angularity as boat's knees, added internal strength. Fastenings of bronze and copper joined parts into whole.

The scene might have emerged from the 19th century. I was in the Apprenticeshop, a branch of the Maine Maritime Museum, where young people wielding hand tools were learning the skills of wooden boatbuilding through a two-year apprenticeship.

"The idea," said Lance Lee, the Apprenticeshop's founder and its director at the time of my visit, "is not to do something for its own sake, but instead to find out why doing things that way worked well. Now that power is rising in cost, we're interested in putting some older solutions into the hands of youth in case they're needed again.

"Getting a craft of any size constructed and under canvas, and involving young people in that experience regardless of the risks involved, is crucial to the continuity of our maritime skills."

Those skills, for Lee, include work and resourcefulness, words he used often during our talk in Bath. Not long after my visit, he left the Museum's Apprenticeshop and opened a similar shop at Rockport. A man of seemingly boundless stamina, a former Marine Corps officer and an Outward Bound instructor, he spoke without wistfulness of the "pragmatic genius" of the 19th century, for he sees its revival around him.

"Apprentices here work in an unforgiving material, wood, that lays down some rules, and you've got to adhere to those rules. The best of man's tricks and nature's tricks are combined in a wooden boat: design evolution, looking at how a shape moves through the water and improving it the next time. Gasoline engines changed all that." And, he added, "there are so many aspects of the human story that get into wooden boats. The people who built those boats were the same people who used them."

They were boats with sonorous, almost exotic names: Muscongus Bay sloop, Crotch Island pinky, Phippsburg Hampton, Piscataqua River wherry, Nomans Land boats. There were catboats, melon seeds, and duckers. Lance Lee speaks of them collectively as a "small craft harvest" and, individually, as stories of progress in a civilization.

Take the humble peapod—usually rowed, occasionally rigged for sailing. "There must be 50 varieties along the Maine coast," he told me. "Our best guess is that they were derived from the Indian *(Continued on page 121)*

Encore for the grace of a bygone era: Eagle *heels to port in a light Atlantic breeze. Built in the 1930s as a training ship for the German navy, she joined the U. S. Coast Guard after World War II. Her steel hull and masts, bark rig, and great press of sail recall the grain ships that rounded Cape Horn early in the 1900s—the twilight of commercial sail.*

FOLLOWING PAGES: *Memories of youthful years under sail fill the mind of Spike Africa, veteran of the last days of Pacific lumber schooners. Bottles sheathed in the macrame he learned as a seaman fill his home near Seattle, Washington. The five-gallon "Texas jigger," at left, and smaller "captain's jugs" come with hanging loops for shipboard wall pegs.*

birchbark canoe." They were built in the winter when the weather was too wild for fishing and obviously unsuitable for farming. "You built boats and you kept warm, of course, by the sheer energy of driving a smoothing plane," he went on. "The variety came into these boats because of different sea and weather conditions. Out around Matinicus, for instance, it's all open, exposed water—from there to Spain. The best fishing is close in to the rocks. Swells come in and swirl around those ledges, so you want a boat that's very maneuverable. You also have to be able to stand up, lean over, and pull up a 70-pound lobster trap.

"The peapod we're building here now has the old 'cod's head, mackerel tail' configuration. That means a very full forward section and a very fine one aft: It's related to the belief that the way a boat leaves the water is more important than the way she enters it."

The peapod, like most Apprenticeshop-built boats, would be sold as a pleasure craft. An exception, under construction in a nearby shed, was a 40-foot Maine pinky. She would be kept by the Apprenticeshop to provide sailing experience and income by freight hauling. I stood ankle-deep in wood shavings and watched an apprentice drive bolts through her keel with a spike set dating from the 1800s. Nearby, the Apprenticeshop's master boatbuilder, Dave Foster, was giving another apprentice a lesson in reading—reading the grain of wood to find its maximum strength.

Trial and error is a common theme. There were no architects to design such workboats, I was told, and no government commissions to draw plans. The boats were too common; and when trends changed there were few blueprints left to guide builders, often resulting in the extinction of a type. To forestall further loss, apprentices scour the Maine coast for old craft and old-timers' knowledge. The knowledge becomes part of the learning process; boats acquired are displayed "as is" in facilities of the Maine Maritime Museum.

Most graduates of the Apprenticeshop continue to build boats. Largely, they stick to wood; in commercial yards or in the silence of old sheds they ride the revival of interest in handmade objects. A few make a philosophical leap to fiberglass. But as Lance Lee says, "We're romantics here. Otherwise we'd be working down at Bath Iron Works."

Romance: In sailing a traditional ship, it is undeniable. And though every traditional craft tells a special tale one of the most romantic belongs to the Baltimore clipper. For me, a two-day sail on the *Pride of Baltimore* brought that story to life. She is a lean topsail schooner with tall, raking masts and a great spread of sail. She is a vessel of hardwood and handmade fittings, with sails of cotton and flax, and manila rigging. With her unabashed beauty and historic message, she advertises Baltimore—as business place and tourist stop—at ports on both coasts, the Great Lakes, and the Caribbean. Not a copy of an actual vessel, she is, say her creators, simply "another in a series."

Time-honored skills enjoy a revival in Bath, a boatbuilding center in Maine since the 17th century. At the Apprenticeshop, where young people learn to craft wooden boats by hand, Mary Jane Hammel fits a cap rail to form the gunwale of a Grand Banks dory.

The original Baltimore clippers were once among the fastest, most intrepid sailers on the sea—"the highest development of small American sailing craft," wrote the naval historian Howard Irving Chapelle. They were conceived in 18th-century Chesapeake Bay yards by shipwrights who discarded European notions of design in a quest for speed.

Speed meant survival, for the Colonies' trading ships were constantly threatened by armed vessels of warring European powers. Later, in the Revolutionary War, the states were critically dependent on fast blockade-runners. With the War of 1812 came a heyday for privateers—privately owned vessels armed and commissioned to prey on enemy merchantmen. Many of the privateers were the swift Baltimore clippers. They so annoyed the British that in 1814 the Royal Navy attempted an invasion of Baltimore to rout them out. The attack failed; observing the battle, young Francis Scott Key penned the "Star Spangled Banner."

In the peace that followed, Baltimore clippers turned to smuggling, pirating, and the notorious slave trade. By the mid-19th century, they had passed from the scene, giving way to more capacious ships.

As I sailed from Jacksonville, Florida, to Savannah, Georgia, I wondered what a 19th-century seaman would think of this latest Baltimore clipper. He would, no doubt, find the *Pride,* with her crew of 12, surprisingly uncrowded. In the War of 1812 a privateer of her length—90 feet on deck—might have packed a hundred men on board. They would include a skilled crew for complex maneuvers plus additional men as replacements for casualties and for prize crews. I tried to imagine a hundred people living on the *Pride* for weeks

or months at a time—and couldn't. Space was at a premium: I slept on the floor or borrowed the bunk of a crew member standing watch; the *Pride* has no passenger facilities.

The 19th-century sailor might have found the crew's routine familiar. Always, there is the helm to be manned. Decks need swabbing, sails need setting, lines need hauling, and gear needs repairing.

The crew divides into two watches. On our first day out I joined the starboard watch: 6 a.m. until noon, and again from 6 p.m. until 10. In the evening I took a turn at the tiller. The breeze had picked up; staysail, fore, and mainsail were set. The sea was pink in the setting sun; then the western sky settled into long flat streaks of orange and purple. We seemed to be flying: almost ten knots, on a reach, heeling to the wind.

Later, I made my way below decks. In the hold, night gaped down the hatch. My eye traveled upward, through the hatch and up 87 feet of foremast, adzed from Douglas fir, to where the moon bobbed on the masthead. There was nothing to remind me of the 20th century. The sounds were the crispness of wind stiffening sails and water rushing beneath the hull, and the occasional groan of a line. The sights were of another time: spars and sails under star-filled sky.

"Look over the bow," said deckhand Gary Surosky as I joined him on watch. He noted the whiteness of the churning water, a measure of our speed. "They say, 'She has a bone in her teeth.'"

For Gary, a college graduate, sailing the *Pride* meant a practical education. It meant getting along with people in a sometimes trying environment. "Teamwork is essential," he told me. "If you're up there on the yards and someone suddenly steps off the footrope without informing adjacent mates, it's dangerous for everyone else."

Teamwork aloft was an aerial ballet the next afternoon as we approached Savannah. Without hesitation, crew members scampered up the rigging and edged their way out on yards 61 feet up to furl sails. Moving out along the bowsprit, other deckhands looked like agile spiders in a familiar web.

Sleepy watermen along the Savannah River saw the *Pride* and were startled by the sound of her cannons. Knots of people gathered along Savannah's 250-year-old waterfront to watch her dock. Her message, it seemed, belonged not only to Baltimore, but also to Savannah and every other city awakening to the pride of its maritime past.

That awakening takes different forms. A 19th-century seaport setting has been created at Mystic, Connecticut, and it has become one of the nation's premier maritime museums. Elsewhere, local groups or developers have brought new life to long-neglected waterfronts. And a handful of old ports preserve the past simply through the continuation of maritime traditions and livelihoods.

New Bedford, Massachusetts, is such a place. In the mid-19th century it was the greatest whaling port in the world, successor to Nantucket in that distinction. Whaling *was* New Bedford: "Yes; all these brave houses and flowery gardens came from the Atlantic, Pacific, and Indian oceans," wrote Herman Melville in *Moby Dick*. "One and all, they were harpooned and dragged up hither from the bottom of the sea." And in New Bedford, the author had heard, fathers "give whales for dowers to their daughters, and portion off their nieces with a few porpoises a-piece."

All of that began to change in the latter part of the 19th century. Petroleum superseded whale oil as a source of illumination. During the Civil War, Confederate raiders destroyed many whalers, and the North sank old ones to blockade southern harbors. Textiles took over New Bedford's economy. When that industry failed in the 1920s, New Bedford slumped. Harvesting the sea had all but died out; then in the 1960s the city was sparked by the idea of reviving its economy—and its heritage—by turning again to the ocean's bounty. A new hurricane barrier had made the port storm-safe; rehabilitation and development transformed the waterfront. Today New Bedford is the leading commercial fishing port on the East Coast.

Early one morning I attended New Bedford's daily fish auction. Outside, trawlers, laden with their catches, rode low in the water; fishermen huddled in the falling snow. Inside, in a small, smoky room, I stood among men just in from a week or more at the fishing grounds. Their weathered faces bore the stamp of many immigrant cultures; the names of their boats and a description of their catches were chalked on a board. A bell sounded, followed by shouting, scribbling, tense whispering, and more bells. That morning, about a quarter of a million dollars' worth of business was done.

Later, I walked the stone-paved streets of the restored waterfront district, a National Historic Landmark, where beautiful buildings from the whaling era stand near grubby seamen's bars. The juxtaposition reflects the approach to preservation of the city's Waterfront Historic Area League (WHALE), whose John

Maritime Lore
at Mystic Seaport

Bullard says, "Whaling is gone, but fishing is its descendant; New Bedford is a functioning seaport and not just a museum."

Transient seamen may still find inexpensive lodgings at the Mariner's Home, which opened its doors in 1857. In the entranceway I noticed the rates: rooms, $5; shower only, $1. The home is not open to the public, but its director, Ron Hansen, offered to take me next door to the Seamen's Bethel, a chapel in continuous use since 1832. The chapel's prow-shaped pulpit is reminiscent of sailing ships. Eloquent cenotaphs march around the walls. One eulogizes Capt. William Swain of Nantucket: "This worthy man, after fastning to a whale, was carried overboard by the line and drowned" in 1844. Another speaks of William Kirkwood of Boston, who in 1850 "fell from aloft, off Cape Horn, and was drowned." In 1863 Charles Petty was killed by a shark. Other cenotaphs poignantly recall boats and crews lost at sea as recently as 1980. Ron paused in front of one and in the long list of names pointed out his father's.

The closest thing New Bedford has to a whaler these days is a meticulous half-scale model in its Whaling Museum. Mystic Seaport Museum owns the wooden whaler *Charles W. Morgan,* one of the last survivors of the great hunting ships of the 18th and 19th centuries. They were prosaic vessels; no one thought much about preserving them in their time. So, also, with countless other sailing ships.

When the British bark *Elissa* called at Galveston, Texas, in the 1880s little notice was taken. The far-ranging three-master was but one of hundreds of ships that arrived during Galveston's glory years between 1870 and 1900. It was the largest port west of New Orleans and the seat of a financial empire based on the export of cotton and the import of manufactured goods, which, carried inland by rail, helped build the entire Southwest.

In 1974, as part of a large-scale restoration project, the Galveston Historical Foundation was looking for a sailing ship with ties to the city's past, for use as a museum. *Elissa,* it turned out, was the only known candidate. Over the years she had sailed under many flags and owners. Now she was in the Mediterranean; she had been operating as a cigarette smuggler's motorship, transmogrified almost beyond recognition—and perilously close to the scrap heap. Galveston bought her anyway. In 1977 a restoration crew traveled to Greece and made the hundred-year-old ship seaworthy. Two years later *Elissa* was towed across the Atlantic to Galveston.

When I visited her at a city pier, she looked incongruous amid mammoth freighters and sturdy shrimpers. Shell, keelson, and beams had been restored. She had new decks of Douglas fir; new masts, yards, and rigging pointed skyward. Gleaming teak rails swept around her, complementing her teak companionway. *Elissa's* bow had been restored to the sleekness that was a hallmark of her maker, Alexander Hall and Co., of Scotland.

Hall built ships to the highest standards of the day, a fact that accounts for *Elissa's* longevity. "They knew what they were doing," said Walter Rybka, director of the restoration

"Whaleboat drill" at Mystic Seaport Museum displays the harpoon's special feature—a toggle head that swivels to lock into its target. Ships and small craft, exhibits, and hands-on demonstrations complement the age-of-sail setting at this village on the Connecticut coast.

effort. The standards of builder and restorer differ, Rybka noted. Hall had built *Elissa* to last about 25 years; the restoration aimed to keep her afloat indefinitely.

The mental rebuilding of *Elissa* had been a long and often painful process for Walter and his staff. Almost none of the original plans were in hand. Walter labored for months over the drawings and photographs of similar vessels, pondering every detail. More than once, lack of funding threatened the project.

"I've been carrying around a picture in my head for five years," Walter told me, "and now I'm watching it become reality. It's a fulfilling thing." As we stood on the pier, he traced *Elissa*'s bow in the air with the crook of his hand. "Look at that," he said. "It's the focal point for all the curves of the ship. And it's the most graceful part of the ship."

His reverence for the nobility of the sailing ship was echoed among the nearly 40 other people participating in the restoration. Mostly young, they had come to Galveston from all over the country. Some brought skills, others had only enthusiasm. "They all have a piece of their soul, and not just their paycheck, in it," said Walter.

Because virtually nothing about *Elissa* is squared, carpentry and joinery demanded craftsmanship of a high order. Curving wood came easily to guitar builder Ed Claxton, on board as ship's carpenter. Joiner Rinn Wright had arrived with more than 20 years of woodworking under his belt. He was building the deckhouse when I visited. "I'd have to call this a 'guesstoration,'" he admitted.

A few blocks from the pier, in the spar loft, I met Brion Toss of Seattle, who was splicing strands of wire into an eye, or loop, for the ship's standing rigging. It appeared to be slow, painstaking work, yet it was only the first step. He would go on to coat the eye with tar, then add layers of twine, burlap, hemp, and leather, and yet more tar in traditional processes known as worming, parceling, serving, and leathering. How long would it take to complete the eye? About a day, Brion replied. And there were hundreds of them in the ship's rigging.

The passion that old sailing ships and their lore inspire has to do with an outward quest, and the lure of distant horizons. River craft, on the other hand, evoke something different: an inward journey, into the heart of the nation. If the oceans were thought to breed character, the rivers bred characters. And the greatest of American rivers, the Mississippi, brought forth characters to match—roisterous, rollicking, larger than life.

First, they were keelboatmen and flatboatmen, working people who migrated west after the Revolution. For the farms in the great river valleys the boatmen transported produce and livestock to riverside markets; cotton, tobacco, sugar, rice, and whiskey continued along the muddy-water Main Street to the international port of New Orleans.

The work was hard, and dangers—currents, snags, river thieves—ever present. Around the rivermen grew traditions of prowess and meanness and, most of all, boasting. One traveler in the early 19th century overheard this from a keelboatman: "I'm from the Lightning Forks of Roaring River. I'm ALL man, save what is wildcat and extra lightning . . . I can out-swim, out-sw'ar, out-jump, out-drink and keep soberer, than any man at Catfish Bend. I'm painfully feroshus. . . ."

Planters, gamblers, immigrants   the era of steamboats added its own complement of types to river life. It arrived on the Mississippi and Ohio Rivers in 1811, when the *New Orleans* steamed down from Pittsburgh to her namesake city. Crowds lined the banks to marvel at her. And nature seemed to acknowledge the event with its own salute: one of the greatest earthquakes in America in historic times, centered at New Madrid, Missouri, on the Mississippi.

By 1860 there were hundreds of steamboats churning the inland waters. The growing web of railroads was already threatening them, but while they lasted steamboats brought great profits to some and good times to many more. They occasionally exploded and they yearned to race. They grew bigger, faster, fancier; "floating palaces," they were called, or "floating wedding cakes."

"They were a unique breed—a Yankee invention—those flat-bottomed boats that could run on a heavy dew," Capt. Fred Way told me. "And they had to, because there was no water in the rivers half the time."

Licensed as a river pilot in 1926, and now in his 80s, Fred Way is America's preeminent riverboat historian.

"The boats all had character back then," said the captain, while his dog, Wrecks, extended a friendly paw to me. "They had great big names painted on them that you could read from a mile off without your glasses.

"And they all had steam whistles, of course, and no two whistles were alike. You could tell the boats apart just by the sound of them, like a person's voice. People bragged that they knew 50 and 60 boats by the sound of their whistles, and I believe it."

As much as anything, it was people who kept Fred Way around the rivers. He recalled hearing that anytime Mark Twain needed a character, he needn't look farther than the river. "Mark Twain was right," the captain told me. "You can run the whole gamut, from the gutter types to those who stand around reciting Shakespeare." They still gather: to reminisce, show off restored stern-wheel towboats, and cheer the contenders at the annual steamboat race on the Ohio during Louisville's Kentucky Derby Week.

Until Captain Way organized one in 1928, there hadn't been a major steamboat race since the *Robert E. Lee* beat the *Natchez* from New Orleans to St. Louis in 1870. Now they are a regular thing, a matter of some honor and great fun, involving the cruise steamer *Delta Queen,* built in 1926, and the excursion boat *Belle of Louisville,* dating from 1914. In 1982 a young upstart, the seven-year-old stern-wheeler *Natchez,* joined the race. Captain Way was there, along with thousands of others crowded along the six-mile course.

Passengers filed on board to the music of the boats' steam calliopes. The *Belle* moved to her starting point at the far side of the river. It was the favored position, with the slackest currents, and no one seemed to know just how the *Belle* had secured it. Then the *Natchez* angled into position in the middle. Finally the *Delta Queen* backed away from the pier. Belching black smoke, she proceeded full speed ahead. When the starting shot sounded, she was a hundred yards ahead. Down in her engine room, I was informed, "The idea is to win, and it doesn't matter how."

Nevertheless, the *Natchez* was gaining fast on the *Queen,* whose passengers shouted and danced to the Dixieland jazz being played on the forward   *(Continued on page 141)*

New planking and thick frames of white oak retrace Morgan's original lines; her shape had sagged due to age and hurricane damage. As she rests on a lift dock, shipwright Gil Bliss checks a stern frame. Chief shipwright Roger Hambidge uses cord and a keen eye for fairing—traditionally, a crucial step in attaining a smoothly curved hull. The five-year task—known as "retopping"—called for some 70,000 board feet of new wood to replace most of Morgan's timbers.

FOLLOWING PAGES: *Stern-faced maid surveys the shipcarver's shop at Mystic, where visitors may see woodcarvings old and new, antique tools, and Larry Anderson at his craft. The sunlit work-in-progress: Larry's eagle sternboard carved of pine.*

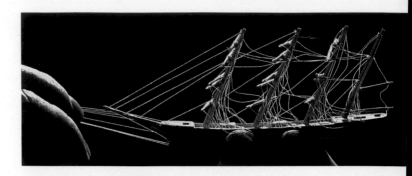

Admiral of
the Minifleet

*Fit for a Lilliputian crew, Erik
Ronnberg's four-masted bark
makes the perilous journey
from maker's hands to glass-
enclosed mooring. "I've had
plenty of shipwrecks," quips
Ronnberg; since the 1940s
he has built hundreds of tiny
models at his home in
Massachusetts. Before that,
as a Swedish merchant officer,
he observed seamen practicing
the craft. His pine-hulled ship,
ready for insertion (above,
at left), carries masts and
yards hinged for handy folding.
With rigging collapsed, the
ship squeezes through the
bottleneck (above, right) into
a sea of painted putty and
harborside detail. After the
putty dries, Ronnberg gently
tugs at stays to raise the
ship's spars. Drops of glue
will secure lines and a rope
stopper will seal the bottle;
a Turk's head knot adds
decorative flair to the work.*

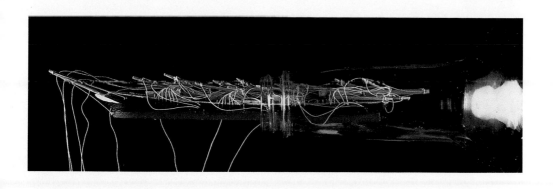

"Yankee racehorse" they called her—the first ship to sea of a new nation's navy. Almost 200 years later Constellation *still inspires pride; in Baltimore exacting restoration preserves many original hallmarks. Long guns—18-pounders—bespeak a fighting career that lasted through the Civil War. Gilt stars on sternboard and enigmatic cat's head on fo'c'sle date from the ship's early days, their meaning a mystery.*

Constellation: *A Tale of Two Centuries*

FOLLOWING PAGES: *Tracery of lights and pennants outlines* Constellation *against nighttime Baltimore. Geometry of modern design glows in the triangle atop the new aquarium. Old and new, shops and dining spots, festivals and street minstrels lure crowds to Baltimore's redeveloped Inner Harbor—the permanent home of* Constellation. *Her launching took place about a mile away in 1797.*

Father of Waters
Hosts a Dowager Queen

deck. The *Natchez* caught up, turned at the markers, and headed back to Louisville. In response, the *Queen* turned early. And the trailing *Belle* had a tugboat waiting to turn her around. In the end the *Natchez* took the victor's gilded horns and the *Delta Queen* came in second. It hardly mattered. When asked what happened, the *Queen*'s Capt. Jim Blum replied, "Just steamboatin'."

No great distance from all the steamboat hoopla, but in marked contrast to it, Richard Kottmyer was simply doing what he always does for his living: ferrying people and cars across the Ohio River between Cincinnati, Ohio, and Constance, Kentucky. His job is also a proud tradition; Kottmyer family ferryboats have made this crossing since 1864.

One afternoon I joined Richard Kottmyer at work. It was the sort of raw, blustery day when the world outside seems an inhospitable place; the two ferries were operating with skeleton crews. We were on the newer ferry, a barge-and-tug operation. A little way off, the other Kottmyer ferry—dating from 1937—kicked up foam with its wooden paddle wheels. As we crossed and recrossed the quarter-mile reach, Richard waved to the regulars from the pilothouse. "They keep coming back, and then their children and grandchildren come," he said. Old-timers still mistake him for his father, Henry.

When Richard's great-grandfather Charles purchased the Anderson Ferry, as it is known, ferries had already been navigating the river for at least 70 years. In many ways the story of the Kottmyer family's ferries is a story of America in microcosm. "My great-grandfather came over from Germany and settled here," said Richard. "First, he was a stagecoach driver. Then he bought a canalboat—in those days there was a canal where the railroad is now. I think he traded his canalboat for the ferry and then bought the landings."

The ferry of 1864 was powered by sweeps. A couple of years later the first Kottmyer-built ferry went into operation—the *Boone,* named for Boone County, Kentucky. The ferry service is one of the oldest businesses in the county. Fashioned of white oak and cypress, the first *Boone* ran on horsepower: two horses walking a wheel-turning treadmill.

Even after the first suspension bridge in the Cincinnati area was built in 1867 the Kottmyers kept building ferries—double-ended and steel-hulled ferries, steam-powered and, later, diesel-powered ferries, a total of seven side-wheelers, all displaying the name *Boone.*

Richard Kottmyer remembers what it was like when he was a boy in the late 1920s: "The farmers would drive their cattle and hogs and sheep from the farms and leave them overnight in fenced lots by the river. Next morning they'd cross and go on to the Union Stockyards—all by foot. We charged a dime a head for the animals."

The fare for cars and foot passengers—a dollar and a dime, respectively—is still the same; but much of the farm traffic now crosses the river on bridges. Ironically, the air age has helped business, for Cincinnati's airport is only a few miles from the ferry landing in Kentucky. Airport workers have been riding

Delta Queen *churns nostalgia up and down the Mississippi and the Ohio, but her native domain lies half a continent away—on the delta of California's Sacramento and San Joaquin Rivers, where she began overnight service in 1927. She first steamed along Ol' Man River in 1947.*

the ferry for 25 years, Richard told me. "Before, people needed the ferry," he said. "Now they use it because they don't like crowded highways. And it's relaxing." Business seemed to be good and since my visit the ferry has been placed in the National Register of Historic Places. But, after four generations, there will be no Kottmyers to take over the business when Richard retires. He has no sons; his sons-in-law and nephews aren't interested. And, he added, Kottmyer ladies have never worked on the boats.

"You couldn't get a stranger to come in and buy the ferryboat," Richard continued. "He wouldn't last a year. You've got to be there every morning and every night. I'm the repairman, bookkeeper, paymaster, welder, president, vice president, everything. People don't want that kind of responsibility now. Whoever wants the ferry can make a living for a long time to come. But who?"

Around the country there are other Richard Kottmyers and Spike Africas and Fred Ways—final links in a chain of maritime tradition. There are many more, though, who are starting afresh in search of that tradition, with interests ranging from figurehead carving in Connecticut to the renovation of Victorian-era houseboats in California.

Sometimes they redefine America's past.

On a golden beach, fringed by rustling palms and Pacific breakers, a sleek, double-hulled canoe gleamed in the Hawaiian sunshine. A dozen boys and men wrestled the craft's curving boom into position; minutes later, with spars and crab claw sail mounted, the canoe was ready for the launching ceremony on the next morning.

It stood for the new and for the old—for America's newest state and for Hawaii's earliest waterborne immigrants, the Polynesians, who arrived here in similar canoes perhaps before the eighth century A.D. Even more, the locally built craft stood for a renaissance of pride among the disaffected of a community drifting between new and old.

The community is Waianae, on the western coast of Oahu, about 25 miles from the highrise hustle of Honolulu. Waianae has little tourism and no industry. On its beaches, though, and in the grooved volcanic hills beyond lies evidence of an ancient culture. Stone platforms were temple sites. Mossy walls mark house sites; terraces were gardens. Petroglyphs remain faintly visible.

Hawaii's first settlers came from islands more than 2,000 miles away, guided by stars, birds, wave patterns, and currents. They were among the world's greatest navigators; their canoes were the center of their culture.

"They relied on their canoes for fishing, for coastal and interisland traveling, and in times of drought, war, or overpopulation for voyages to other islands in the Pacific that they knew of or could discover," says Dr. Kenneth P. Emory, senior anthropologist at Honolulu's Bernice Pauahi Bishop Museum.

The Hawaiians saw their world as an ecosystem, with land and sea inseparable. Their land divisions reflected this. Called *ahupua'a,* these wedge-shaped fiefdoms extended from hilltops down into the ocean, providing total self-sufficiency within their borders.

Then, in the 19th century, came sugar and pineapples—labor-intensive agriculture on a massive scale. The sea lost its primacy. Waianae was the home of a sugarcane plantation, which closed in 1946. Since then, the

area has existed in a cultural and economic limbo characterized by low levels of income and education, high rates of unemployment and crime.

A few years ago Solomon Naone had an idea. Nearly half of Waianae's young people traced at least a part of their origins to the early Hawaiians. Building a canoe of the ancient style might instill a new pride in this heritage. A similar craft had been built on Maui; later, plans for the Waianae craft were derived from the sketches of artists who had accompanied Captain Cook and other European visitors to the Pacific. A public servant who was also chairman of a local historic preservation committee, Sol Naone marshaled funding and enthusiasm for the project.

"This is our last chance," he said quietly as we stood by the canoe the evening before the launching. "The kids around here know good traditional values, but they just haven't wanted to get involved." Supervised by adults, many did become involved, volunteering for tasks such as sanding and sawing. Others were helping with a second double-hulled canoe under construction.

Elsewhere in the community, similar ideas were tentatively beginning to take hold. Working with archaeologists, high school students and dropouts searched for ancient sites and worked at restoring an oceanside temple. A new school program in marine studies was designed to teach students practical skills within the context of traditional Hawaiian culture. Competitions involving large wooden surfboards, of the kind used by ancient Hawaiian royalty, had been reintroduced, and canoe-racing clubs flourished.

Sol Naone saw the double-hulled canoe as "a classroom for the whole community, for sailing and interisland voyaging." He was cautiously optimistic. After months on the beach, where work on it was completed, the canoe had not been touched by the vandalism for which Waianae is notorious.

"The Hawaiian name of the canoe," Sol told me, "is *E Ala.* In English, that means "Awaken!" The next morning, Waianae awoke to perfect weather for the launching. Offshore, outriggers sliced through the water, crew and craft moving as one. Crowds gathered on the beach as the lilting strains of old Hawaiian songs filled the air. Bright leis adorned necklines; fronds decked the 45-foot canoe. Its upper structures were fashioned of spruce and Douglas fir, but the hulls were fiberglass, for *E Ala*'s builders could find no traditional koa logs large enough.

Wearing fern wreaths, *E Ala*'s crew of 12 gathered round to share an offering of ceremonial foods—redfish, mullet, and taro. Benedictions were uttered and a chant rang out. The event was the symbolic severing of the umbilical cord that linked the canoe to the womb of the earth.

Then into the water she went, and with deep strokes her crew paddled out beyond the breakwater.

In the distance, a breeze caught her crab claw sail and filled it. Framed by the vast blue Pacific, canoe and crew might have been a vision of a thousand years ago, of Polynesian voyagers ending their arduous journey in a new island homeland.

The vision might also have been of America: of lands sighted and settled by sea; of inland frontiers explored and nurtured by water; of the people and their vessels that helped the land grow.

As a vision, it was a proud one.

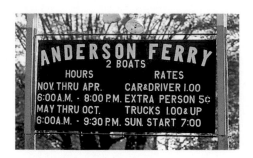

Ohio River institution, the Anderson Ferry means business for Richard Kottmyer—with mascot Josephine—as it has for three generations of his forebears. In dense fog a deckhand readies Kottmyer's 1937 side-wheeler for the five-minute trip between Cincinnati, Ohio, and Constance, Kentucky. Rates have defied inflation: Driver and car in the 1980s pay the same fare charged for a horse and wagon in 1900.

Hawaii: Renaissance of a Maritime Culture

Ceremony and celebration attend the launching of a double-hulled canoe of ancient Hawaiian style. Beyond the breakwater at Waianae on Oahu's west coast the vessel E Ala—Awaken!, in Hawaiian —slices water to the rhythm of paddle strokes; frond-decked crew members later unfurled the crab claw sail to catch wisps of breeze. The canoe's design resembles that of the sleek, twin-hulled craft that brought Polynesian settlers to these isles more than a thousand years ago. But inspiration for the new canoe grew mostly from modern-day concerns: crime and malaise blamed by many on Waianae's alienation from its maritime roots. To counter the trend, civic leaders recruited local youth to help build E Ala as a symbol of awakened pride. Townsfolk and visitors turned out for daylong festivities at the inaugural sail. Among the entertainers: dancers crowned in leis (above), preparing to perform the hula.

Fledgling Days on Wings

Sunset flight in a Stearman over Iowa brings back the grace and glory of the open-cockpit flying

and Wheels

By Tom Melham
Photographs by Stephanie Maze

machines that dazzled the nation during the first decades of the 20th century.

He seemed an unlikely pilot. White of hair, thick of bifocals, and solidly into his 70s, Dale Crites was hardly your daring young man. His flying machine was even more unlikely—a Model D pusher designed by Glenn Curtiss in 1911, only eight years after the Wright brothers' first powered flight.

Like Wilbur and Orville's craft, the Curtiss Model D is an airy collection of struts, wire, and cloth. Looking more like a motorized box kite than an airplane, it seems to grab the slightest wind and go with it like a leaf in a March storm. Its engine, mounted amidships with the propeller pointing aft, "pushes" the craft—hence the designation. In the much more common form, called tractor, front-mounted propellers "pull" ahead.

"Back in 1911 the designers' first objective was to defy the law of gravity," said Dale, smiling as he oiled the engine's rocker arms and the tubes for the aileron cables, then topped the radiator with water. "All they could think of was how to get up in the air. So they made planes light and kite-like."

Then he reached up and gave the propeller a lusty downward snap. Nothing happened. Another snap, and the engine coughed, sputtered, then roared. Dale ran to the crude "cockpit"—a canvas seat strapped atop the forward landing gear like an afterthought—while some friends steadied the wings. The three-quarters-of-a-century-old pilot revved the big V-8, and the plane conceived nearly three-quarters of a century ago shook from nose to tail.

There was a feeling of power, of transformation. Pygmalion was seeing his Galatea coming to life. Gradually the unlikeliness, the oddness of this old couple, melted away. Age lost all importance. Only the afternoon's unpredictable crosswinds mattered, for this man and machine were about to challenge gravity's law.

Dale signaled his impromptu ground crew to let go, and the quivering birdcage in which he sat began to bounce down the grass runway, first no faster than a man might walk. As it reached jogging and then sprinting speed, the shaking steadily worsened.

Suddenly the plane ceased its bucking. It sat back smooth and sleek as any Learjet—and I knew, at that very moment, that Dale's body had taken leave of earth and his soul had begun to soar. Once again, the Curtiss Model D was airborne.

There is a magic to flight, just as there is a magic to any form of motion. We Americans love to move, and we love machines that move us. We especially love old machines, for they carry us not just from here to there, but across plateaus of memory and time.

They take us back to childhood, sometimes to our father's or grandfathers' boyhood days, when such machines were new and toy versions of them burned lasting impressions into young minds. So it is that even in today's space age we still love the rickety old planes and steam locomotives, cable cars and vintage automobiles, trolleys and old bicycles— the wings and wheels of our past.

When I watched Dale Crites fly his Curtiss,

Biplanes rendezvous in stepped-up echelon above the fields of Blakesburg, Iowa, gathering place for antique airplane buffs. The formation consists of a 1927 Waco (foreground), a 1928 Kreider-Reisner, a 1939 Brewster Fleet, a 1929 Parks, a 1931 Bird, and a 1930 Butler Blackhawk.

Busy at restoration, Paul and Deanna Hofacker of Brookville, Ohio, focus on the frame and cowling of a 1934 Waco. Finding parts for such antiques, Paul says, "is a scavenger hunt." He spied this fuselage at a Florida airfield—with goats, ducks, and chickens around it.

it was Oshkosh, Wisconsin, 1981, but it might have been San Diego, California, 1911, near the winter base of the rising young plane maker, Glenn Curtiss. Like the Wrights he had begun as a bicycle maker. Adding power to bikes, Curtiss began to race motorcycles; he set a motorcycle record of 136.3 miles an hour in 1907—five years before any airplane would top 100 mph. He built flying machines with Alexander Graham Bell and the Aerial Experiment Association; in 1909 one of them—the *Silver Dart*—made the first powered flight in Canada, rising from the ice of Baddeck Bay, near Bell's home in Nova Scotia.

One of the obstacles to flying in those days was the Wright brothers themselves. They had solved a major problem of controlling a flying machine, and they took the position that anyone who received money for flying without license from the Wrights was guilty of patent infringement. Legal dogfights between them and Curtiss endured for years.

The Wrights' key patent provided for lateral control—turning left or right. They used a system of lines and pulleys that warped the wings and moved the rudder at the same time. Thus, as the wings changed shape, the aircraft could make smooth, banked turns and then return to level flight.

Curtiss avoided wing-warping. Instead, incorporating a Bell idea, he produced banked turns by attaching movable little wings—*ailerons*, in French—to struts between the two big wings. In time plane makers hinged little wings to the rear edge of main wings, to form the familiar ailerons we know today.

The Navy took to the skies in 1911, acquiring a Curtiss pusher in a version that came to be designated A-1—U. S. Navy airplane No. 1. The following year young John Kaminski of

Milwaukee, Wisconsin, bought a used Model D from Curtiss in San Diego; the $5,000 price tag included flying lessons.

In 1911 Curtiss also issued a manual of sorts: "Should the aeronaut decide to return to terra firma," stated instruction five, "he should close the control valve of the motor. This will cause the apparatus to assume what is known as the 'gliding position,' except in the case of those flying machines which are inherently unstable. These latter will assume the position known as 'involuntary spin' and will return to earth without further action on the part of the aeronaut."

Kaminski christened his biplane *Sweetheart* and went barnstorming with her—briefly. There were few airfields around. In 1914 he took off along a town street in Wisconsin and hit a pole. He survived; *Sweetheart*'s remains wound up in a blacksmith's shop, where they were rediscovered in 1941. Dale Crites bought them in 1957, restored the craft, made 150 flights with her, and gave her to a museum near Milwaukee. In 1974 he crafted a reproduction, *Silver Streak*.

It was *Silver Streak* I watched that day in Oshkosh, rumbling into the air at 35 to 40 miles an hour to cruise at 55, an image from the dawntime of flying.

Locating antique machines is not easy in our throwaway society. Restoring their rusted and rotted exteriors can be even more challenging. But for true believers, it is not so difficult. In fact, it's not even enough. Tom Bins of Three Lakes, Wisconsin, operator of a 1929 Great Lakes biplane explains: "There are a lot of air museums around the country, and some have really good restorations. I'm glad

FOLLOWING PAGES: *"Yellow peril,"
a 1942 Stearman, rides benignly
through a radiant Iowa sky. Its
World War II nickname derives
from its color and the student
pilots who trained in it. Easy
to maneuver, it became a
popular crop duster and a pet
of helmet-and-goggles fliers.*

these planes have been saved, but I hate to see them just hanging under a roof, collecting dust. Planes weren't made to hang—they were made to fly!" Apparently many agree with Bins. Each year tens of thousands of Americans crowd dozens of air shows and fly-ins in hopes of seeing Curtiss Jennys, de Havillands, Waco biplanes, and other antiques take to the air.

The largest air show, sponsored by the Experimental Aircraft Association, occurs annually in Oshkosh. The EAA embraces not only antiques but also the most modern assembly-line productions as well as experimental planes. So many airplanes converge during this week-long fly-in that local Wittman Field temporarily becomes the world's busiest airport, surpassing even Chicago's O'Hare!

Then there is the Antique Airplane Association, which focuses exclusively on old aircraft. Robert L. Taylor, its president, believes that "to take an old piece of machinery, restore it and fly it, that's the ultimate. You've proved that your handiwork, your ability as a mechanic, is good enough to put your life on the line."

Bob Taylor first fell in love with airplanes as a farm boy growing up in the 1930s. "We had all aviation's heroes then—Lindbergh, Earhart, Wiley Post, others," he recalls. Much later, he started buying planes, then a strip of grass in southeastern Iowa, near Blakesburg, where AAA members now congregate annually to renew friendships, to show off their airplanes, and—most of all—to fly. Several large, plain buildings between two runways mimic the look of 1930s hangars. They house a modest aviation museum, offices, and the "Pilot's Pub," its walls lined with broken propellers and broken-down pianos.

Here the spirit of barnstorming still prevails, especially when pilots gather nightly to rehash the day's events over a beer. But right now the Pub is closed. It's early morning, the first full day of the AAA's annual fly-in. The grass is wet with dew, and pilots—dozens of them—are tinkering with engines or zipping into flight suits and jackets festooned with patches proclaiming their loyalties to this airplane club or that plane maker.

Goggles, aviators' helmets, and Snoopy scarves are everywhere. Not only do they minimize the windchill that comes with open-cockpit flying, but they also give the proper dash to a pilot's image—though antiquers tend to cringe at comparisons to Snoopy.

By 8:30 or so, a few pilots have turned from coffee and scuttlebutt to their morning exercises, doing some lazy eights or barrel rolls in the blue sky overhead. There is no agenda, no air show, no competition; fliers fly when they feel like it. All is as relaxed as the 1930s—or at least as the thirties *seem* to have been from the perspective of our day.

"Of course," Taylor says, "the thirties were very different. We're kidding ourselves if we think we can ever go back. But here the airplanes are the same, the skills in flying and repairing are the same, the enthusiasm and the romance are the same."

It is the economics that differ. In 1929, a hundred different airplane companies existed in the U. S. alone. Today there are about a dozen. This, Taylor argues, is one reason why older planes have so much character and are so distinctive—while modern small planes, much like modern cars, look alike.

And how do they perform? AAA member Tom Lowe, a commercial airline pilot who flies a Boeing 737 *(Continued on page 161)*

Fighting Men and Their Flying Machines

World War I aces Ray Brooks and Kenneth Porter remember the dogfights of more than half a century ago amid the early warplanes and other craft at Old Rhinebeck Aerodrome in upstate New York. Brooks sits on a 1918 Model T Ford, beside the shooting star insignia he designed. It first emblazoned the Spads of the 22nd Aero Squadron, which Brooks joined in deadly dogfights over France in 1918. Six of his targets went down. Porter scored eight kills before his 21st birthday. Just behind the 1942 Fleet starting up (opposite) stands a British Sopwith Camel with roundel marking; Sopwiths logged more kills than any other plane of World War I. The Fleet boasts a tubular-steel fuselage—a framework made popular by fast-climbing Fokkers in 1918. No American-designed plane fought in the Great War, but many combat fliers trained in Curtiss Jennys—such as the one behind the Model T. Brooks and Porter each flew some 50 hours of solo before they sortied for battle. On one patrol eight Fokkers boxed in Brooks and riddled his craft. His back grazed, he landed safely, itching to return. "My patriotism in those days was 100 percent," he recalls. "I expected nothing but to die."

Horizon tilts as Cole Palen banks into a slow roll in a 1931 Great Lakes—a versatile aerobatic biplane that can fly upside down with ease. Palen continues the flying circus tradition at Rhinebeck, as stunt pilots duplicate the spins, rolls, and other crowd-pleasers of barnstorming days. Mock dogfights feature a copy of a 1917 Fokker triplane (opposite), the type flown by Germany's ace of aces, Manfred von Richthofen.

The Vintage Days
of Motoring

for pay and a 40-year-old biplane for fun, offers to take me up in the latter. It's a yellow Stearman with U. S. Navy markings as a reminder that it was a Navy trainer in World War II. In the 1940s, a dozen miles from here, hundreds of Stearmans like this one swarmed to and from the Navy air station at Ottumwa. The "yellow perils" painted the skies with slips and stalls and spins, wingovers and loops and snap rolls, and wobbly V-formations—the syllabus of fledglings.

I get in the forward cockpit, strap on the snug helmet and seat belt, and look around—for 360 degrees. The plane is open, so different from the glass-encased isolation of most modern aircraft. In the Stearman I'm still outdoors. I can smell the air, feel the sun and wind. It seems strange to sit in front of the pilot. Tom assures me this is normal; the advantage of the back cockpit is its location behind both wings, where Tom can see even more than I can up front.

We taxi to the end of the runway in use, a grassy lane that slopes unevenly downward, ending not very far away in a field of shoulder-high corn. The engine roar is deafening, but suddenly I hear something even louder—and look up to see another plane drop out of the sky, its wheels just clearing our top wing before it lightly touches down. I am shaken, and immediately recall that Blakesburg has no controllers, no tower, no radio. Tom, not startled at all, had seen the plane coming from his rear seat.

We begin to roll over the grass, racing jerkily toward the wall of corn. From my front-row seat it's easy to imagine the propeller chewing through cornstalks like a Roto-Rooter. Mercifully, the cornfield falls away just in time. We're in the air!

As we slowly circle the field below, a hawk comes near, so close that I can almost count its tail feathers. We hold the same speed for a few moments; then Tom opens the throttle, and the hawk appears to soar backward.

There is an enormous feeling of involvement in the Stearman. It rides the air the same way a sports car holds to curving country roads; it reacts, feeling its way through winds rather than flattening them out. At times, invisible currents toy with us, making the Stearman waver, sideslip, bubble up, or sink without warning. My stomach is on an elevator ride, and there's nothing to grab onto—except my faith in Tom Lowe's expertise.

He starts us into a slow roll: The right side tips up, and I stare ahead, watching the horizon turn 360 degrees like the sweep hand of an office clock. My brain may know better, but emotion insists that the surroundings are spinning, not the Stearman.

We start a loop. It is absolutely terrifying—the horizon falls away and suddenly the sky is green, the land blue. I am upside down in a wide-open cockpit. Although the centrifugal force actually rivets me to the seat, to my mind all that prevents me from falling out is one very tight seat belt—and ten white-knuckled fingers braced against the sides of the cockpit.

Gradually we pull out of the loop, and the universe returns to normal. Thoughts turn to

Under the lindens and over the shiny cobbles, a 1928 Pontiac rolls into the Vanderbilt Museum on Long Island—once the home of transportation tycoon William K. Vanderbilt II. In 1904 he began the Vanderbilt Cup Race—the nation's earliest annual auto race of international note.

NATIONAL GEOGRAPHIC PHOTOGRAPHER JOSEPH H. BAILEY

long-ago summer nights on Coney Island, riding the Cyclone. Both that roller coaster and this roller-coaster-without-rails deal in the twilight realm between terror and exhilaration, between fear and fun. Like mountain climbing, they excite the senses, fostering a self-control born of self-abandonment.

Aerial thrills and chills of a different sort regularly take place near the Hudson Valley town of Rhinebeck, New York. Every weekend, May through October, the Old Rhinebeck Aerodrome lures audiences to its bleacher-lined airstrip, where World War I Spads, Fokkers, and Sopwiths take to the air and do battle just as they did in 1917. They are all European craft—French, German, English; there are no American machines in the warplane group. We came late to World War I, and even before 1914 European technology had forged ahead—despite the Wright brothers' historic first. When the U. S. Army entered the war in 1917, its air service had no combat craft among its 200-odd planes.

Mixed in with the dogfights and aerobatics at Rhinebeck is a measure of old-time melodrama, usually centering on the villainous Black Baron, who each weekend puts heroine Trudy Truelove through perils that Pauline never dreamed of. Here is blonde Trudy, crudely accosted by the Baron for a kiss. Here she is, tied to an airplane wing and taken aloft, then dropped, in effigy, into a haystack.

So it goes for poor Trudy until one of her heroes arrives in his Sopwith biplane and challenges the villain to aerial combat. The Baron takes off in his Fokker DR-1 triplane, the type favored by Germany's most celebrated World War I ace, "Red Baron" Manfred von Richthofen. At first the exceptionally maneuverable triplane closely tails the Sopwith, its twin Spandau machine guns crackling threateningly. But soon the hero turns tables on the Baron, fires a burst, and black smoke streams from the DR-1 as it loses altitude and "crashes" just out of sight of the crowd.

It is only a show, yet with an echo of history. On April 21, 1918, while closing on one Sopwith Camel in his triplane, von Richthofen was jumped by another Sopwith and met his end—though it's debatable whether the Sopwith or ground fire downed him.

The Black Baron, however, survives his defeat as he does every weekend, and soon is happily signing autographs. Behind his sooty exterior stands the Aerodrome's stocky, round-faced, and rather Mickey Rooneyish creator, Cole Palen. His face often wears a light spattering of oil, for antique rotary engines do not recycle their lubricant as newer engines do, but gradually spray it out on airplane and pilot. This was one reason, Palen explains, why aviators wore those long, dashing scarves—they could grab them easily, to wipe oily goggles and faces.

To them, "oil" usually meant castor oil, preferred for rotary engines because it stuck so tenaciously to bare metal. It wasn't always preferred by the pilots, however.

"On long flights," says Palen, "pilots would get so much castor oil fumes in their faces that they would succumb to its laxative effects. But these were resourceful men, and they soon found an antidote—blackberry brandy." Hence the popularity, somewhat fabled, of this drink, which not only counteracted castor oil but also gave fliers a dose of liquid courage, Palen claims. True or not, the stories flow like blackberry brandy as Palen points out some planes that didn't participate in today's show.

Jaunty 1925 Stutz joins the Glidden Tour, a reliability and endurance test first run in 1905. The 1912 Packard wheel (right) flaunts spokes of hickory. The tire's long air stem often leaked on bouncy roads.

FOLLOWING PAGES: *In dusters and long summer dresses Glidden Tour members re-create an early 1900s picnic in Stony Brook, New York. Mostly Fords and Packards line the curb. A 1912 Buick rests on the grass.*

Here is a 1911 Blériot XI, an American duplicate of the French plane that first conquered the English Channel. There sits a copy of a 1910 Hanriot, looking for all the world like a racing shell with wings instead of oars. Apparently its designers figured that, since both air and water are fluids, a boat would cleave the sky as neatly as it did a lake. Well, the Hanriot flies, but not *that* well.

Palen explains: "Every plane manufacturer in the early 1900s had different ideas on how to design an airplane. They were still experimenting with where to put the engine, or the tail, or whatever.

"Each maker had his own control system, too, which makes flying them a mess. You see, you fly a plane like you ride a bicycle; reflexes take over. Once your reflexes get set on the Hanriot and you switch to say, the Curtiss, or the Blériot, or Nieuport—you're lost."

Getting "lost" is easy in Rhinebeck; of the 60 different airplanes Palen has acquired, none came with an operator's manual. Most arrived as wrecks—scrounged from warehouses, hangars, and barns, picked up at auctions, or received as gifts. Thousands of man-hours go into restoring each plane: replacing missing sections and rotten struts, rebuilding the engine, puzzling out peculiar controls, encasing wings and fuselage in a new suit of cloth. Then comes the final challenge: getting this former pile of junk to fly.

No restoration is truly final, however, for the fabric covering will age. It may last as long as 20 years, or it may need replacing after 10. Then a new cloth skin must be cut, applied, doped, and painted. It is tedious work.

Some people may consider such work a sort of child's play, a throwback to the balsa-wood-and-tissue-paper models many of us built when we were kids, then rapidly outgrew. True, Palen has not outgrown that childlike love. His middle-aged body is still full of boyish enthusiasm and wonder. You can see it in the way he tunes an engine or plans the day's aerial acts or just reminisces about the time he wandered into an old barn and found beneath some dusty cloths the time-ravaged remains of an extremely rare biplane, an American-made 1909 Voisin.

"It was like going up to a haymow and seeing the radiator of a Rolls-Royce poking out," Palen recalls. He bought it, of course. "It's the only original Voisin around," he exclaims, his joy as boundless as that of a kid on his first bicycle, for Cole Palen is a walking celebration of the child that dwells within us all.

Too often, 20th-century man tries to imprison this inner child with fear and logic: We must "grow up," "get a job," "quit playing around." But even when we follow such advice, the child inside may ultimately triumph. Take Jack Lambert, who heads a technical instruments company in upstate New York. He is in his 50s, successful, with a flair for glen plaid suits. His business is business—but his passion is old automobiles.

"The only difference between men and boys," Lambert maintains, "is the size of their toys." His favorite plaything is a 1909 Lambert (no relation) touring car, one of only five known in the world. It was produced by John William Lambert, a largely unsung pioneer in the feverishly creative years of the 1880s and '90s. European automobile inventors had made solid gains, bicyclists had stirred a national clamor for good roads, and farmers yearned for an *(Continued on page 175)*

Rain keeps a Tin Lizzie under wraps at the Glidden Tour on Long Island. The 1917 Ford displays a black, steel-shell radiator. It replaced the brass radiators of earlier Model Ts, such as the 1913 flivver shown opposite with its owner, *William Dolan of Norway, Maine. Its driver's side has no door; to get to the wheel, the driver crosses the passenger side. Henry Ford produced the Model T, his "car for the people," from 1908 to 1927— more than 15 million all told.*

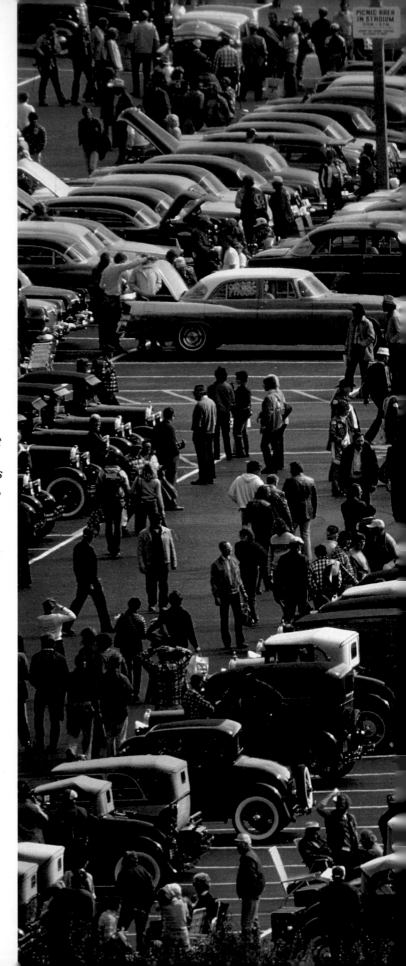

Show time: Spruced-up autos come to judgment at the Antique Automobile Club of America meet in Hershey, Pennsylvania. The annual event draws more than a thousand entries, including the world's largest gathering of antique autos. The judges, some 500 strong, scrutinize each machine for authenticity of detail. Rust, dirt, chipped paint, or faulty wiring also cost points. Major classes include pre-1930 antiques, later models produced at least 25 years ago, and the classic cars—those with special distinction based on style, size, cost, and numbers produced. This group boasts such elites as the La Salle, Pierce-Arrow, and Rolls-Royce. Model A Fords, arrayed in foreground, merit a special class because of their popularity. The four-day meet also features a flea market for spare parts such as hubcaps, grilles, and fenders.

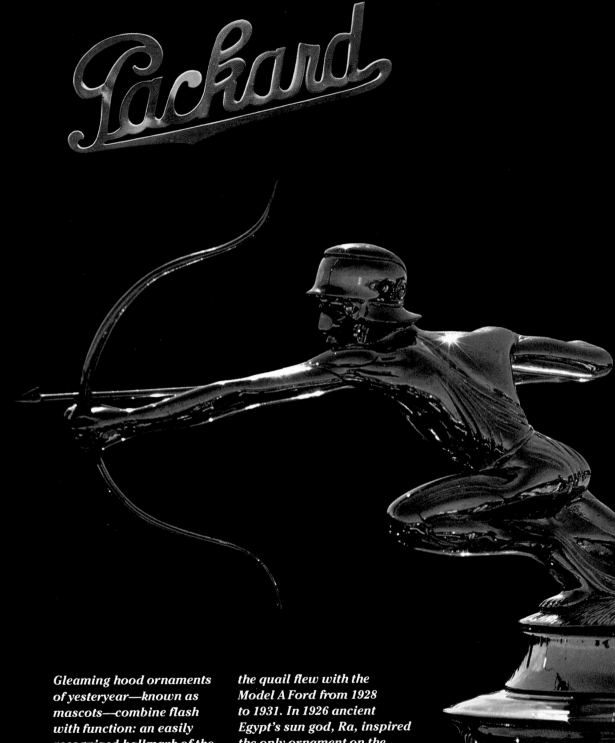

Packard

Gleaming hood ornaments of yesteryear—known as mascots—combine flash with function: an easily recognized hallmark of the maker and a handle for the radiator cap as well. Helmeted archer guarded the 1928 and 1929 Pierce-Arrow. The speedy the quail flew with the Model A Ford from 1928 to 1931. In 1926 ancient Egypt's sun god, Ra, inspired the only ornament on the Stutz. Script adorned the Packard grille from 1904 to 1929. The owner of a Daimler displayed the first mascot in 1896—aptly enough, an

Power, Elegance, Excellence

One of the most powerful six-cylinder cars in its day, a Twin Valve Six McFarlan mirrors elegance and engineering excellence at the landmark Bella Vista farm and distillery in West Virginia. Crafted in 1922, the McFarlan boasts a 120-horsepower engine with 24 valves, 18 spark plugs, and two independent ignition systems described as "the most sure-fire, double-guarded setup ever heard of." In top gear it can reach 76 miles an hour, but with its iron-head engine and thick steel chassis it guzzles a gallon of gas about every eight miles. The taste for luxury spawned many small, independent makers that hand-tooled distinctive cars: Cunningham, Templar, the Wills Sainte Claire Gray Goose. One specialty model, the Davis Parkmobile, came with wheeled jacks that enabled it to squeeze sideways into tight parking spots. When the stock market crashed in 1929, so did much of the market for quality-crafted cars.

alternative that would free them from the freight rates set by railroad monopolies.

There is some evidence for the claim that John William Lambert was driving his first gas-powered car in Ohio in 1891. This is two years before the Duryea brothers built what was generally credited as the first successful gasoline automobile in America.

I met Jack and his Lambert on the Glidden Tour, a week-long event for members of the Antique Automobile Club of America and the Veteran Motor Car Club of America. Each year they explore a different part of the country in vintage cars. Past itineraries have included terrains as challenging as Colorado's Pikes Peak and New Hampshire's Mount Washington; the one I joined focused on less exhausting Long Island.

Monday morning, and the parking lot of the Smithtown Sheraton was buzzing with 235 antique and classic autos. Owners labored over balky engines, drove back and forth in cars aglow with brass and enamel, buffed fingerprints off bumpers. Some wore dusters and caps; some were millionaires, yet traces of grease often blackened their hands.

All had a weakness for massive headlamps, varnished wood trim, tufted leather seats, and other reminders of an automotive age when studied richness was standard equipment. When car wheels were shaped from wood and were carefully pin-striped, not mass-produced from metal. When fenders curved gracefully down to meet brass-edged running boards. When radiator caps evolved into miniature works of art that embodied each automaker's distinctive style. Even the company names were evocative, and still they conjure up images of grandness and speed: Pierce-Arrow. Stevens-Duryea. Duesenberg.

A pair of silver-haired gentlemen entered the parking lot and strolled with obvious joy through a part of their past. Talk turned to magnetos and hand spark advances, planetary transmissions and carbide lamps, and other once vital devices now long obsolete.

"Remember how these things used to go when we were kids?" one asked as they gazed fondly at an old Chrysler. "Oh, they still go—some of them," the other replied.

Indeed they do, for the Glidden Tour emphasizes performance. The name stems from an early supporter of the auto industry. Charles J. Glidden made three global tours by auto. On one roadless leg, from Minneapolis, Minnesota, to Vancouver, British Columbia, he drove 1,800 miles on railroad tracks, his car fitted with flanged wheels. With the American Automobile Association he promoted touring from 1905 to 1913 as a means of popularizing the auto and proving it could compete with horse-drawn vehicles. His yearly Tours were endurance runs, all but one covering more than a thousand miles.

Today's Glidden Tour revivals are not so strenuous. Half of them have not exceeded 500 miles, and today's roads are far better. Yet the challenge and the emphasis on performance remain. Many cars at the Sheraton are

With Gary Woodward's expertise, the car he "brought home in bushel baskets" takes shape as a 1914 Cadillac in Ann Arbor, Michigan. The 1912 Cadillac had the first electric self-starter; in place of cranking, it began the auto's "part in the emancipation of women," wrote one chronicler.

old enough to have entered the early Tours, and all—from a one-cylinder Cadillac to a 12-cylinder Packard—work. Each day they follow a prescribed route. Checkpoints along the way mark their progress.

"Checkpoints, schmeckpoints," said Jack Lambert. "We're all here to have a good time." I had joined him to share the good times in his maroon-and-brass Lambert and as navigator to the day's goal: Southampton some 40 miles distant. As the 2-cylinder, 235-cubic-inch engine chugged away, Jack asked a friend if he needed a ride.

"No, thanks. I've got good clothes on," came the grinning reply. I would have reason to remember his words, but at the time we just laughed and, with a throaty *honk-honk* of the horn, set off down wooded country roads.

You don't get inside a Lambert, you climb up on it. Like other antique autos, it rides high, with more physical and psychological distance from the road than modern cars have. Because it's roofless, you also have a lot more headroom and visibility. Another advantage is its speed, or lack of it—about 40 miles an hour tops.

"Fast enough to get there but slow enough to see it," said Jack. Although newer cars breezed by us, they seemed insignificant, their roofs barely reaching our knees. The Lambert was above the clutter, a moving observation platform, not just a capsule for shuttling people from here to there. I wondered aloud why Jack's friend declined a ride: "Was the Lambert prone to breakdowns? What had given out so far?"

"Everything," Jack said with a grin. "The axle broke one time. I didn't even know it until I turned to the side of the road and saw my left rear wheel go rolling past."

"What about replacement parts, Jack? How do you get a new axle for a 72-year-old car?"

"What you can't find, you make. Just remember that if somebody made it once, you can make it again. There's nothing you can't fix." Only two days earlier, he had made a gasket from cardboard. When a starter switch refused to work, his on-the-road repair consisted of "sanding" corrosion off the contacts by rubbing them on the macadam.

Then Jack talked about the air-cooled Franklin motorcar, soundly built but prone to overheat; in the days of dirt roads, dust and bugs clogged the engine's cooling fins.

"You had to stop often and clean the fins. One way around this was to wait till you got to the top of a hill, leave it in gear, open the throttle wide, and turn off the ignition. Now you're going downhill and the engine is gulping in all the air it can get—through the carburetor—and the air is cooling the engine from the inside. Of course, you're also pumping the exhaust system full of raw gasoline. You get to the bottom of the hill, turn the switch back on, and *ka-blooey!* A number of cars were set on fire that way."

I am glad the Lambert is water-cooled.

The Lambert, by the way, is no weak sister. It conquered Pikes Peak on a previous Glidden Tour, emerging in better shape than its owner, who several times nearly passed out while cranking the engine at 12,000 feet.

A few miles down the road, our problem was not altitude but a sharp *clunk* under our feet. Jack pulled over; off came his tie, shirt, and glen plaid suit coat. He crawled under the car, emerging a few minutes later with a greasy T-shirt and bad news: A metal retainer on the transmission had snapped. Everything still worked, but the transmission surely would deteriorate under the stress of driving. We were near Patchogue, a town large enough to have a welder who could patch the bit of broken metal. Half an hour or so, I suggested, and we'd be back on the road. No such luck, Jack moaned. "You can't take off the transmission without first taking off the entire car body. You can't take off the body without taking off the steering column, and you can't take off the steering column without taking off the radiator—so it's really a job." What we needed, he decided, was not a welder but a machinist, who could create a whole new part that could be installed without first tearing the Lambert to pieces.

Fate and several gas station attendants soon steered us to a machine shop, littered with old engines and scrap metal. The heavyset proprietor looked at us and the Lambert as if we were all part of some fantastic mirage he knew he should ignore. Jack verbally designed the needed part; the machinist said his shop was geared more for boring out V-8s, but he would try. An hour or so.

Nine hours—of gasoline-alley small talk and delays—later we staggered out of the shop with a retainer. Southampton was impossible; dusk made even our return to the motel a challenge, for the Lambert's carbide lights weren't operational. A motorist in a modern car escorted us all the way back.

The next day, problems turn from mechanical to meteorological. A classic nor'easter has slammed into Long Island, and the Lambert—like many of its contemporaries—is hardly more weatherproof than a bicycle. It lacks not only windshield wipers, but also a windshield. Its only concession to the elements is a folding top with "curtains"—partitions with clear panels that hang down over the car's open front and sides. They flap in the wind and hinder your view, but they keep most of the rain outside—or at least transfer it from your face to your feet.

There are other drawbacks in stormy weather. Shortly after we set out, Jack has an ominous announcement: "There go the brakes. I've seen them stay wet for two weeks." Then a reassuring grin. "I can still stop, though, by using the transmission."

And so we chug on, Jack working the brakes against the engine to heat them up and dry them out. But the rain continues. Soon our friction-drive transmission gets wet and starts to slip. Then one cylinder cuts out. Still we keep going, running on the remaining one. Then—*boom*—a terrific backfire, and our engine is dead. We roll to the roadside and get out into the rain. We have no brakes, no transmission, no engine. Jack valiantly tries to restart the Lambert, but ultimately he must do what he has never done on 21 Glidden Tours—call a wrecker.

The following morning breaks raw and wet. Yet off go the Gliddenites. Among the treasures remaining in the lot is the Lambert, looking sad, its plastic tarp blown back. I ask Jack why he takes his rare antique on the road, repeatedly risking damage.

"Ego gratification," he says grinning. "Why do people run a marathon? I think it's a form of death. But they do it, again and again."

When the tour ends, Jack wins an award for his skill in keeping the car going. He accepts, predictably attired in a glen plaid, but I will always remember him in that grease-streaked T-shirt, flat on his back beneath the defiant workings of his car.

The Long Life Span of a Covered Bridge

Similar tenacity in spite of hardships—and, some would say, common sense—has saved more than vintage automobiles. In 1978 concerned citizens of Sheffield, Massachusetts, were warned that the town's best-known antique—the Sheffield covered bridge—was about to fall into the Housatonic River.

Bridges, especially wooden ones, take a beating from sun, weather, vandals, and time. It was to protect the bridge timbers from damp rot and summer sun that builders originally roofed spans—not to keep the snow out, as many people surmise. Indeed, in the old days snow had to be hauled in to make the bridges usable by horse-drawn sleds.

Sheffield folk had fond memories of their 93-foot-long bridge. They remembered it as a place of refuge in a storm, a fine height for diving in swimming season, a place to park and court. By 1978 it had stood for more than 140 years, and though much repaired, had acquired a definite swayback.

Experts were summoned; repair estimates hovered at $50,000—a lot for a town of only 2,700. But the community rallied round the sagging span, raising more than half the needed amount through donations, auctions, and even postcard sales. A matching federal grant put Sheffield over the top. Restorers removed the bridge to shore up its stone abutments, renovated and straightened its wooden truss supports, then returned the bridge to its original location. Workmen had laid a new roof of cedar boards and a floor of oak planks, same as the original in 1837.

Similar grit has helped save some antique railroads. Doomed by diesels and changing economics, steam locomotives might have lapsed into extinction decades ago were it not for dedicated rail buffs. For example, when the Denver and Rio Grande Western Railroad planned to abandon one of its narrow-gauge steam operations in 1967, railfans across the country convinced Colorado and New Mexico to purchase the run and operate it as a tourist attraction. Rechristened the Cumbres and Toltec Scenic Railroad, the segment follows 64 miles of track originally spiked down a century ago to serve silver camps in the San Juans, a range of the Rockies.

Chama, in northern New Mexico, is the western terminus where, from June through October, 60-year-old iron horses come to life. Today engine No. 487, a 12-wheeled Mikado model, sits on the siding, its single headlamp aglow. Its name derives from the fact that the Baldwin Locomotive Works built the first of the type for export to Japan.

Dark smoke streams skyward from the straight stack of No. 487. Escaping steam softly whistles through a relief valve. Every minute or two, the air compressor pistons hammer out a ponderous *lub-dup*, like a giant, living heart. There is more to No. 487 than bolts and boiler plate. The locomotive, of course, is magnet *(Continued on page 187)*

Sheffield's covered bridge, the oldest in Massachusetts, perches on cratelike cribbing at the Housatonic River. Guided by tradition, noted "bridgewright" Milton Graton restored the 1837 span with framing chisels, wooden pins—treenails or trunnels—for nails, and this rustic crane, or gin pole. The bridge rode back on timber tracks to straddle its stream once more.

FOLLOWING PAGES: *Frozen in time, the 1832 Bath Bridge spans the Ammonoosuc in New Hampshire.*

Make Way
for the Tricycles

Freewheeling family trio, the Sandersons parade their tricycles during a Wheelmen's club rally on Mackinac Island, Michigan—Bessie leading in a reproduced 1885 Cheylesmore, Harvey at the handlebars of an 1888 Humber, and daughter Doris Woodward pedaling an 1886 Rudge Coventry Rotary with a high wheel on her left and two small wheels on the right. Near Defiance, Ohio, Lowell Kennedy and his wife and son (opposite) operate the nation's only family repair shop exclusively for antique cycles. Pneumatic tires, rack-and-pinion steering—19th-century innovations for cycles—helped autos progress. As women took to cycling, skirts grew shorter and Amelia Bloomer's bold innovation gained popularity.

New Life for Cable Cars
in San Francisco

Another cable car makes the grade on Hyde Street, steepest hill in San Francisco's world-famous system. Started in 1873, cable cars ended the agony of horses that had hauled the predecessors. These cars travel by gripping a moving underground cable. Packed Powell Street cars (above and right) reflect the system's heavy patronage. In 1982 the cars halted for major repairs, a job that would silence the familiar clanging bells for two years.

Rail Buffs Recapture
the Days of the Iron Horse

and muscle of any train. Few tourists come to gape at the converted boxcars that stretch out behind. People cluster around No. 487; some dream of riding "up front" with the fireman and engineer. To me the cab seems dark and hellish, its iron walls and ceiling blackened with a launderer's nightmare of soot, coal dust, smoke, oil, and grease.

Each morning the fireman enters this chamber of horrors to build a new head of steam. Often he emerges looking like a tryout for an old-time minstrel show, his soot-blackened face streaked with sweat.

A few minutes before departure, engineer George Knauff and fireman Earl Knoob again board No. 487. Not much daylight penetrates the grimy front windows, and eyes accustomed to the bright Rocky Mountain sun need time to adjust. Suddenly there is a blast of light and of blast-furnace heat as Earl opens the firebox door to stoke the fire. George checks his watch and pulls the whistle cord four times, signaling, "all aboard."

"Highball!"—railroadese for "Let's go!"—shouts Earl. George shoves a lever forward, clangs the engine's bell, adds throttle, and the steam pistons go: *Chuff! Chuff! Chuff—Chuff—Chuff.* And the train begins to move.

Soon out of Chama it encounters the steepest part of its run, a 4 percent, 14-mile-long grade up to Cumbres Pass. A steady rain of ash and cinders streams in through open windows. No wonder the crew wears not only trainman's bib overalls, caps, and gloves, but also safety glasses. Within minutes, hair, clothes, and skin are gritty.

Earl is steadily scooping up coal from the tender, pivoting, pitching it into the firebox. He pauses only to check steam and water gauges. The climb up to the pass consumes 3,500 gallons of water.

George is intent on a dozen levers and valves at the front of the cab. There is no steering wheel. Trains go wherever the rails take them, but the engineer must adjust continually for curves and grade changes. He eases off the throttle here, spreads more sand on the track there (to increase traction between steel wheels and steel rails). Since each adjustment is followed by a lag of several seconds, he must anticipate the needs in advance. He also must have a good ear for when his engine is slowing down or speeding up.

Seventy minutes after leaving Chama, No. 487 reaches 10,015-foot-high Cumbres Pass, high spot of the line, which ends at Antonito, Colorado. Earl has shoveled some two and a half tons of coal. Neither man has had much chance to take in the aspen-dotted vistas along the winding course. Now, heading downhill, Earl can enjoy the view, which becomes increasingly convoluted as it nears magnificent Toltec Gorge. Accompanying the scenery are the incessant clickety-clacks, whine of wheels forced into a tight turn, *psssst* of air let out of the brakes—all background rhythms in the railroader's symphony.

Unlike the Cumbres and Toltec, most of the short line steam railroads operating in the nation today are standard-gauge, their rails spanning 56½ inches. The most common narrow-gauge is 36 inches. The East Broad

Devotees volunteer their skills at the Castro Point Railway Museum in Richmond, California, to strip away the patina and rebuild a 1922 Baldwin, symbol of the days when steam engines— stacks puffing, whistles wailing, and rods flashing—made rails hum from coast to coast.

Top Railroad, a narrow-gauge line based in Rockhill Furnace, in south-central Pennsylvania, is unique in that it is almost intact.

In addition to steam locomotives and rolling stock that were in use when it regularly hauled passengers and freight, the EBT boasts an eight-stall roundhouse and turntable, a foundry, steam-driven machine and carpentry shops—enough in fact to build its own railroad cars, which is exactly what the company did for years.

Says operating vice president Roy Wilburn, "Everything is original, and most everything works." The EBT even maintains its own coal mines, prized for more than a century for their almost smokeless coal. Coal was the company's prime freight, hauled to iron smelters at Rockhill Furnace, or to the Pennsylvania Railroad main line in nearby Mount Union.

Chartered in 1856, the East Broad Top closed its doors a hundred years later, selling out to a salvage company that eventually restored part of the line rather than scrap it. Today the "Eastie" remains America's oldest operating narrow-gauge line east of the Mississippi, a National Historic Landmark. People who took a ride on the EBT 20 years ago as kids are coming back now with *their* kids, says Wilburn. They ride in vintage style. Car Number 8 offers seats of red plush in elegant, cast-iron frames. Walnut and bird's-eye maple grace its detailed interior.

Pride of the fleet is EBT's parlor car, fitted with observation platforms. Inside, mother-of-pearl call buttons and ornate wall sconces alternate with heavily beveled windows. Wood columns, wicker chairs, and carved trim recall an age that may have lacked our trillion-dollar GNP but was in some ways far grander. It was an era attuned more to

comfort than to speed, one that considered travel an adventure, not mere motion.

The patrons who could afford such comforts in time turned to airplanes and helicopters. Today, however, some executives are rediscovering the private car and preferring its luxuries to the faster but in many ways more spartan airplanes.

C. Victor Thornton, board chairman of a steel fabricating firm in Fort Worth, used to fly his own corporate airplane but "never got the kick out of flying that I get out of *Imperial*"— his private railroad car.

"With your own car, you stand out," Thornton told me. "I call it 'land cruising' because it's like having your own miniature ocean liner. Just ring for a drink or sit on the back platform and get a suntan or play bridge or watch the scenery go by."

Today some 500 railroad passenger cars in America are owned by individuals, museums, clubs, and corporations. About 140 are true "private cars" designed for individual rather than public use—and only some 50 of those are running. Their owners call them "private varnish" for the lustrous finish that sets them off from workaday cars.

Thornton's *Imperial,* built in 1925 for the officers of the Santa Fe, is one of these. From rear to front, it features an observation platform, lounge, three staterooms, full bath, dining room, crew's quarters and bath, pantry, and kitchen. Bureaus, vanities, beds, and other furniture are built-in and compact. The decor is Art Deco—blond oak paneling, accented with nickel-plated hardware, mirrors, clear plastic drawer pulls, and milk-glass light fixtures. Thornton has added some Santa Fe furnishings and memorabilia.

The overall effect is simple elegance,

reflecting the fashion of the Roaring Twenties, when steam railroading and private cars rolled to the final peak of their golden age. Most of Thornton's major modifications have concerned not the car's basic looks but its basic systems: He replaced steam heat with propane, converted ice chests to refrigeration, and expanded the car's electrical system to handle stereos, a microwave oven, even his daughter's curling iron.

Of course, private railroad cars are not for the low-income set. *Imperial's* array of storage batteries cost $8,000. Thornton paid another $12,000 to have modern couplers installed—and could have spent twice as much if he hadn't bought used ones and had his own company do the installation.

"It's expensive," Thornton readily admits. "But motor homes can now cost $60,000—so paying $100,000 or even $200,000 for a private car isn't so bad, when you consider what you're getting."

Just what *do* you get? A lot of comfort and room. And a lot of attention, says Thornton. More people have sought him out because of this car than because of his business connections or his civic or fraternal groups. The luxurious car also enables its owner to become an active member of the American Association of Private Railroad Car Owners, which each year picks a convention site, makes up a "consist," or train, of private cars, and hires Amtrak or some other carrier to haul the assemblage on a tour.

One recent year the Association decided to go south of the border, meeting in Mexico City. Amtrak trains set out from California and Illinois, picking up private cars along the way.

The spirit resembled that of a neighborhood house tour—if your neighborhood happens to be Park Avenue.

Owners proudly showed each car's particular amenities and decor. Visitors oohed and aahed appropriately. It didn't really matter that this Amtrak special was nearly half a day late at San Antonio; the train was the party, and the party had begun. Not long after *Imperial* was coupled onto the consist, its white-jacketed attendant, Gus Newman, was taking drink orders. Thornton's guests circulated between lounge and platform, where they could watch the reddening curtain come down on another Texas sunset as they hurtled smoothly along at 75 or 80 miles an hour.

A five-course dinner followed in *Imperial's* dining room, starting with shrimp cocktail and ending with homemade lime-icebox pie. Afterward I excused myself and returned to the platform, to enjoy a cigar under the stars and mull over the day's experiences.

I had learned that some private-car owners observe "black-tie-after-six" and other rules almost as dated as the cars themselves. Call it snobbery or style, such on-board rituals help re-create a way of life that otherwise no longer exists—a past that, in fact, most of these private-car owners never had, for they grew up after railroading's golden age. Theirs is a nostalgia once removed.

I turned and saw Vic Thornton appear on *Imperial's* observation platform. He gazed at the cloudless night, then out at the steel rails shimmering faintly in the starlight.

"Is there any better way to travel?" he asked, beaming.

Not for my money, I thought. If only I had enough of it to buy, renovate, and maintain my *own* private varnish.

Plume of coal smoke billows from the throat of Engine No. 90 as it rumbles past Cherry Hill crossing (opposite), midpoint of the Strasburg line. Sash windows in the cars open to give passengers a clear view of the rich Lancaster County farmland. Here dwell the Amish, members of a religious sect who till the fertile fields without mechanization and rank among the nation's most productive farmers. Above, No. 90 chugs by its Pullman-built open observation coach to recouple for the next departure. Fully loaded, the tender can hold 18½ tons of coal, each ton fueling a round trip.

Grimy jobs from railroading's smoke-and-cinder days: A hostler at Strasburg wipes clean the side rod that powers a white-trimmed driver of Engine No. 90. The wheels, each more than 4½ feet tall, can carry the locomotive to a top speed of 50 miles an hour. In the cab (opposite) a fireman stokes the bituminous coal blazing in the firebox. The boiler must build up an intense head of steam—200 pounds of pressure per square inch— to budge the 106-ton engine.

FOLLOWING PAGES: *Whoosh! Blowing overnight damp from its mechanical lungs, the fired-up iron horse prepares for work.*

Notes on Contributors

Exploring the traditions of seafaring came agreeably to LESLIE ALLEN, after a recent assignment for the Special Publication *Secret Corners of the World* took her to Cape Horn and its trove of maritime history. She made her first Atlantic crossing by ocean liner at age three, with her parents on Foreign Service assignment. On the Special Publications staff since 1978, she will contribute a chapter to the forthcoming *America's Hidden Corners.*

IRA BLOCK ranged from Maine to Oahu to photograph the story of maritime preservation. He traveled mostly by jet, but a change in sailing time led him to an open-sea rendezvous with the Coast Guard training ship *Eagle*—a rare adventure for a small-boat angler whose outboard never leaves the sight of land. Based in New York, Ira has free-lanced several assignments for the Society, including the Special Publication *Back Roads America.*

Free-lance photographer ANNIE GRIFFITHS was born in Minneapolis, majored in photojournalism at the University of Minnesota there, and still lives in her native city. On assignment for Special Publications she photographed the north woods of her home state for *Exploring America's Backcountry,* the Colorado Rockies for *America's Magnificent Mountains,* and rural preservation for this volume. Her work will also appear in *America's Hidden Corners.*

ETHAN HOFFMAN served as a photographic intern at the Society in 1976. Since then he has contributed photographs both to NATIONAL GEOGRAPHIC and Special Publications—and to *Life, Geo,* and the *New York Times Magazine.* He spent four months working in a Washington State penitentiary, then coauthored *Concrete Mama,* a book on prison life. He graduated from the University of Missouri and currently free-lances from New York.

STEPHANIE MAZE, who photographed the chapter on transportation, grew up in Germany, began her college education in Paris, and completed it as a language major at Georgetown University. She began work at the Society as a translator, left to become a news photographer in San Francisco, then returned to Washington, D. C., to free-lance. She has photographed for NATIONAL GEOGRAPHIC in Mexico, Spain, and Puerto Rico.

The assignment to explore the world of antique wheels and wings coincided with TOM MELHAM's own efforts to preserve a bit of America's past. In his spare time he has renovated a century-old Victorian town house in Washington, D. C. A dozen years at National Geographic have taken him to distant coral reefs, the monuments of ancient Egypt, and the wild lands of our West. His Special Publications credits include a chapter in *The Desert Realm,* and authorship of *John Muir's Wild America.* He is writing several chapters for the forthcoming *Alaska's Magnificent Parklands.*

H. ROBERT MORRISON's childhood in a village amid central Ohio's rolling farmlands gave him an appreciation for both the hard work and the rewards of tilling the soil. His study of the farm life of an earlier America reinforced the impressions of his youth. He graduated from Howard University in 1969; as a member of the Special Publications staff he has contributed to *Mysteries of the Ancient World, America's Magnificent Mountains, The Ocean Realm,* and *America's Majestic Canyons,* and coauthored *America's Atlantic Isles.*

GENE S. STUART grew up in South Carolina, her regional interests nurtured by local history and the oral traditions of a large family. She studied literature and art at the University of South Carolina and archaeology and art history in graduate school at the University of Georgia. With her archaeologist husband she coauthored the Special Publications *Discovering Man's Past in the Americas* and *The Mysterious Maya.* She wrote *The Mighty Aztecs* and contributed a chapter to *Mysteries of the Ancient World.* She has written children's books on American Indians and archaeology.

STEPHANIE MAZE

At yesteryear's pace a tourist carriage visits restored homes of Philadelphia's Society Hill. Such houses, sunk into decay, faced destruction until preservationists saved them. Now they take a proud place as neighbors to Independence Hall and Penn's Landing, where William Penn first stepped ashore in 1682.

Composition for *Preserving America's Past* by National Geographic's Photographic Services, Carl M. Shrader, Director, Lawrence F. Ludwig, Assistant Director. Printed and bound by Holladay-Tyler Printing Corp., Rockville, Md. Color separations by the Lanman Progressive Co., Washington, D. C.; Lincoln Graphics, Inc., Cherry Hill, N. J.; N.E.C., Inc., Nashville, Tenn.

Library of Congress CIP Data:

Main entry under title:

Preserving America's past.

 Bibliography: p.
 Includes index.
 1. Historic sites—United States—Conservation and restoration—Addresses, essays, lectures.   2. United States—History, Local—Addresses, essays, lectures.
 I. National Geographic Society (U. S.).   Special Publications Division.
 E159.P74   1983   973   81-48076
 ISBN 0-87044-415-8
 ISBN 0-87044-420-4 (lib. bdg.)

Index

Acknowledgments

The Special Publications Division is grateful for the opportunity to share the expertise and enthusiasm of America's preservationists—amateur, academic, and professional. Many of them are cited in the book; we are especially thankful to the National Trust for Historic Preservation and to Harry C. Allendorfer, Jr., Paul E. Garber, William J. Murtagh, John T. Schlebecker, Phinizy Spalding, Roger B. White, and William L. Withuhn.

The Louis Armstrong cornet on page 86 was photographed by courtesy of the New Orleans Jazz Club Collections of the Louisiana State Museum.

Additional Reading

NATIONAL GEOGRAPHIC has vividly portrayed historic sites and cities and other themes related to preservation; check the cumulative index. Among other periodicals much of interest was gleaned from the National Trust's *Historic Preservation* and from *American Preservation.* The following works provided general background and information on architectural styles and urban preservation: Alice Cromie, *Restored Towns and Historic Districts of America;* James Marston Fitch, *Historic Preservation;* Charles B. Hosmer, Jr., *Presence of the Past* and *Preservation Comes of Age;* John Poppeliers, S. Allen Chambers, and Nancy B. Schwartz, *What Style Is It?;* Nathan Weinberg, *Preservation in American Towns and Cities.* For our section on farm life of the past we were helped by such books as Richard Paul Hinkle, *Napa Valley Wine Book;* Leland L. Sage, *A History of Iowa;* John T. Schlebecker and Gale E. Peterson, *Living Historical Farms Handbook;* Frank Waters, *Book of the Hopi.* For maritime preservation our references included Robert G. Albion, William A. Baker, and Benjamin W. Labaree, *New England and the Sea;* William Avery Baker, *A Maritime History of Bath, Maine and the Kennebec River Region;* Howard Irving Chapelle, *The Baltimore Clipper;* Eloise Engle and Arnold S. Lott, *America's Maritime Heritage;* Ray Samuel, Leonard V. Huber, and Warren C. Ogden, *Tales of the Mississippi;* Mark Twain, *Life on the Mississippi.* We found interesting material on transportation in the following works: Automobile Quarterly Inc., *The American Car Since 1775;* Peter M. Bowers, *Curtiss Aircraft 1907-1947;* Richard Burns Carson, *The Olympian Cars;* Empire State Railway Museum, Inc., *Steam Passenger Service Directory;* Charles H. Gibbs-Smith, *The Aeroplane;* Milton S. Graton, *The Last of the Covered Bridge Builders;* Clarence P. Hornung, *Wheels Across America;* Stephen W. Sears, *The American Heritage History of the Automobile in America;* David Weitzman, *Traces of the Past.*